IGNORE THE IMPOSSIBLE

Larry,

You rock.

www.mascotbooks.com

IGNORE THE IMPOSSIBLE

For more information, please contact:
Mascot Books
620 Herndon Parkway #320
Herndon, VA 20170
info@mascotbooks.com

Library of Congress Control Number: 2019913856

CPSIA Code: PRV1219A
ISBN: 978-1-64543-311-8

Printed in the United States

IGNORE THE IMPOSSIBLE

DANE RAUSCHENBERG

CONTENTS

INTRODUCTION

W hy does the world need another motivational book?

Well, frankly, the reason I decided to pen this how-to guide was because I feel too many of these types of books in circulation are extremely lacking. What they often promise is false hope couched in pabulum to titillate the mind, but in the end, they offer no substance. They prey on people who are desperately searching for assistance. They offer the bare minimum of an inkling of a solution when people fervently want ideas on how to change their lives for the better. This type of hook isn't followed by every book out there, but more than enough exist for me to have seen it numerous times and get bothered by it just as often.

You see, in order to catch the eyes of prospective readers, these books have to come up with a new system, or a new catchphrase, or some sort of "secret." They must create something that no one else has made before so they can show how different they are. Like many a snake oil salesman who insists their drink or powder is the elixir to create a better life, these books must have an idea of the one true way to solve your problems, as the concerned reader. However, the fact remains that if anyone anywhere is telling you, without knowing what your situation is, that they have the ultimate answer to all your problems—they are trying to sell you something.

Now, let me tell you how to solve all your problems.

I'm kidding. This opening may see a tad harsh or abrasive. I do not mean for it be that way. What I want to impart upon you, a person who has invested their money and time into reading my words, is that I plan to pull no punches in this book. I promise you I will not advise you to do anything that I haven't myself made the decision to do. This will not be a "Do as I say, not as I do" book. What I will do is provide for you a framework for a way of life that can help make your own existence better. We are so unique, and our situations so diverse, that any one way offered to solve the problems of everyone must be so vague as to be worthless. I will not be offering vagueness.

This book is not the answer to all your problems. What this book is, however, is a collection of ideas, methods, and hints that I have learned through personal experience or gleaned from others. I feel these ideas can assist you in creating the best possible version of yourself that you can. I make you no promises. I don't think I can solve everything. But when I saw a gaping hole in the literature out there on how to convey the ideas presented within these pages, I felt it was my duty to fill that breach. The opening statements I made may come across as jarring. I speak as such, as I wish for all to grasp from the start here that I will not refrain from telling you what I think works for you and when you should avoid common advice that is actually quite harmful.

Having said all of that, what makes me so special to impart such pearls of wisdom? What you should know first and foremost about me is I have always been rather unimpressed with myself. When I have achieved something of note, even something that has never been done before, I more or less assume I was the first to do so simply because no one else tried. For example, I once ran a twelve-hour race in Erie, Pennsylvania, just one month after my second marathon ever. For half a day, participants run around a one-mile loop to see how far they can go in that time limit. Unlike races with a distance to run, this tests how you can handle a race that has no finish line, only a clock. When the day was over, I had finished first by a large margin and had broken the course record.

While pleased with my effort, I was hardly over the moon. I figured that beating a record in a town like Erie, which was hardly a hotbed of running records, meant that I just had bested a few runners who showed up now and then to run some loops. I didn't know that the record was over twenty years old. In addition, I wasn't aware that the locations of some of the most infamous races out there are often in smaller out-of-the-way areas. Often, it is the fact that the race is off the beaten path a bit that is part of the allure. So besting a two-decades-old record is impressive anywhere you do it. In fact, in the fifteen years since I ran those eighty-four miles in twelve hours (the equivalent of an 8:34 mile for half a day), no one has come closer than seventy-seven miles to the record I set. I've come to accept that the record I hold is at least one of note. It is far from unbreakable but solid nonetheless.[1]

Even after I made a name for myself by running the fifty-two marathons in fifty-two consecutive weekends, almost averaging a time that would qualify me for the Boston Marathon with each event, I was never one to consider myself an expert on running. But time and time again, I would see other people with far fewer credentials claiming they were just that. Similarly, I also noticed that often in the motivational and inspirational world, people collected five-figure speaking engagement fees talking to a group about their success. The irony was the only real success they had achieved was—wait for it—getting people to pay them five-figure salaries to talk about how they had become successful. Quite the pair of serpents swallowing each other's tails, right? I guess in some sense, that is some sort of achievement, but it wasn't the one upon which I wanted to base my foundation.

My previous books have often been called inspirational and motivational, even though they weren't necessarily meant to be. I was basically relaying my adventures and attempting to regale others with tales of mirth. Hopefully, these stories would entertain, and if people could derive the success I had achieved athletically into some formula to drive them forward with their own lives, then that was a bonus. Sometimes I would encounter

---

1 Made even more noteworthy because until that day, I had never run one inch past 26.2 miles. As you will see later on, ignorance truly can be bliss. Also, welcome to my footnotes. Here you will find oodles of random thoughts and asides. Venture within at your own risk. Thar be dragons.

someone who was a bit dismissive of my books, saying that they wouldn't be able to apply the lessons within to their own desires because they "weren't a runner." They felt there wasn't really a direct corollary from what I had done to what they wanted to do with their own lives. While I felt that was folly—as why must everything be a direct one-to-one correlation in order to inspire?—I decided I wanted to find a way to reach everyone, regardless of how they classified themselves. But I barely felt like I had it together. How could I possibly be telling others what to do?

However, as time went on, I realized that I at least had some life lessons that no one else had. Since I cannot tell you how many times I have done things in what seems to be the longest or hardest possible way, where I wish someone else had given me some guidance, I knew at the very least I could help people learn from my mistakes. I have always felt that information that is not shared is completely wasted. As such, I finally bit the bullet and put down onto paper the ways in which I think I can help you ignore the impossible.

So what does *ignore the impossible* mean? I am not saying that you can do anything that you want. In fact, that's where I think most people in this line of business feed you a load of malarkey.[2] If we face reality, we learn there are truly many things we cannot do. I have tried and tried and tried, but I simply cannot dunk a basketball. I have tiny hands that can't palm it and have no leaping ability. However, having said that, the only way we can find out what we can do is by ignoring what we think our limits are and striving to do more. This does not mean throwing all caution to the wind. This is not saying you should ignore advice from those who have done more. This is saying the best way to find out how far you can go is to go further than you've ever gone before. Simple, right?

---

2   I am over forty now, so I like to use old-man words. *Get off my lawn!*

> *Most of the important things in the world have been*
> *accomplished by people who have kept on trying*
> *when there seemed to be no hope at all.*
> — Dale Carnegie

Success is never guaranteed. But by doing nothing, failure absolutely is. So please enjoy the fruits of my failure. Within this book are the ways in which I feel you can make the best of everything you have. You may agree with many or just a few of them. I can say that at one time or another, I probably disagreed with all of them myself. That is why I made the mistakes I did. From those mistakes comes the realization that if I had done things differently, my life would have been easier. So, rather than regret that I didn't do them then, I am making the positive decision to continue to do them for the rest of my life. This book contains the tools I use and the lessons from which I hope to build the best me possible.

With them, I know you, too, will learn to ignore the impossible.

CHAPTER 1

THINK OUTSIDE THE HIPPO

If you are alive, you have heard the phrase "think outside the box." For that, I apologize. This oft-used expression was obviously original at one point, but that time has long since passed. We now need a new idiom for a new time. I humbly submit, for your approval, that everyone should instead begin using "think outside the hippo." Why? Let me explain.

By now you have probably heard that hippos are more dangerous than virtually every other animal in Africa. While exact numbers of deaths are not known, hippopotamuses rival crocodiles for human fatalities throughout this massive continent. Let's just say for the sake of moving on that I am not going to dispute that crocodiles kill more people. I will allow crocs the top spot. But think about how dangerous an animal has to be in order to even be in the discussion with crocodiles![3] This really isn't surprising when you think about these water horses. Hippos are ten-thousand-pound, aggressive, unpredictable beasts, with no fear of humans, possessing razor-sharp foot-and-a-half long teeth. Egad!

Yet at the same time, these killing machines allow at least four different types of fish to clean and repair certain parts of their bodies. In addition,

---

3   Lions aren't even close. The so-called kings of the jungle—which don't live in any jungles, so that tells you how dumb humans are when it comes to naming things— kill just a measly one hundred or so people a year.

oxpecker birds are permitted, in flocks, to remove ticks off the hippos' hides.[4] So while a description like the one above would give you the impression that no animal could come anywhere near a hippo, lest it be devoured or ground into dust, it is not uncommon to see these animals resting quietly while schools of fish and flocks of birds scour them clean.

Furthermore, while they are massive, hippos are also quite fleet of foot, being able to gallop nearly 30 miles per hour on land. Moreover, they also swim startlingly fast—although they actually don't really swim, as their feet never really leave the bottom; they actually just do a series of porpoise-like leaps off the bottom.[5] I will not be offended if you dog-ear this book right here, pull up YouTube, and look for the one well-known video of this dark hump pursuing a boat in some lake only to erupt out of nowhere with the gaping maw of a ticked-off hippo chasing the boat. It is terrifying.

Yet, despite all of this, everyone loves hippos.[6] We love them when they are hungry, hungry marble-snuffling hippos. We love them when they are Baby Fiona of the Cincinnati Zoo, photobombing couples getting married through the glass of her enclosure. We love them when they are escaped pets of drug lord Pablo Escobar flourishing in the main river of Colombia, the Magdalena, where a quarter-of-a-century experiment has been going on to see what an extinct megafauna might do to a foreign environment.[7]

In other words, if there was ever an animal that has defied its rotund nature to be extremely fearsome, while at the same time defying that fearsomeness to still be beloved, it is the hippo. If there is anything that is more outside the box than that, I don't know what it is. So I propose henceforth, whenever you want to come up with a different way of thinking, you simply think outside the hippo. We good? Good.

---

4   Although, at the same time, these birds suck blood from open sores, which means they are at least mildly parasitic as well as in mutually beneficial relationships. By now you are completely confused by what kind of book this is. That's OK; I am too.
5   Yep, hippos are like dolphins.
6   Take that, Ray Romano.
7   This is 100 percent true. Seriously, hippos, everyone! Let's hear it!

Now that we have the phrase established, let's talk about how to implement it.

> *Somewhere, something incredible is waiting to be known.*
> — Carl Sagan

The absolute first thing to do to change the way you have done something before is to refuse to accept "Well, that's the way it has always been done" as a reason for not changing. By itself, there is no reason with less punch than "tradition." No innovation, no truly groundbreaking event, no change that has propelled the human race forward was done by people who weren't challenging the status quo. We often get annoyed when children ask "Why?" when "Why?" is the truest of all questions. Why we do something is far more important than virtually anything else. It is the engine. It is the combustion that propels us forward. Don't get me wrong—often we have no answer to the question of why. But it doesn't mean it shouldn't be asked.

So act like a child, at least when it comes to wonderment and the tackling of problems. Children often have an ignorance of convention. They don't know how things are supposed to be done, so they just figure out a way to get it done. Let me give you an example.

I once had a leaky faucet, a two-handed kind, with the hot and cold controlled by separate handles. The cold handle would leak whenever it was used. But it wouldn't do so right when you used it. It would wait, like a water ninja, until long after I had left and was not around to sop it up with a towel. This leaking water would pool on the sink, and after a while, it would run down the length of the top of basin and then finally collect on the wooden tabletop connected to the sink. This would stain the wood as it pooled. Eventually it would seep through the wood or find a crack somewhere else and drip down onto the floor. There the water would cause yuckiness under the sink where another cabinet made it difficult to see the water immediately and clean it up. Since it didn't immediately leak when the handle was turned off, it was impossible to just stand there and wipe it away. Short of calling a plumber to fix the handle, I was at a loss as to how to solve this problem.

I tried a variety of different things to stop the leak—tightening this, loosening that, cursing furiously at the sink, and so on. I randomly mentioned the problem while I was shooting the breeze with a friend. His young son suggested a simple solution that would at least fix the immediate problem. Instead of worrying about the leak itself, I should handle the water. If I could divert the water when it pooled and run it back into the basin instead, the staining and eventual drip onto the floor wouldn't be a problem. He was right. I put a big glob of superglue on the basin in the way of the water, creating a levee of sorts. The water would drip out sporadically, pool for a bit, hit the superglue, and then run down into the sink. Problem solved. That was months ago.

I never bothered to fix the handle.

Looking at a task in a different way is how you invite randomness. Randomness is where you will inevitably get a slew of ideas that don't fit what you need at first blush. However, often in that stack of possibilities is the eventual solution, or at least the next step on the road to the solution you need. In reality, little is truly random or chaotic anyway. The outcome of a coin flip—the epitome of randomness—can actually be predicted if you break down how much pressure is being applied to flip the coin, what side the coin started on, air turbulence, and other factors. Yet we don't need randomness often to help us make a decision. Merely thinking about the potential randomness gets your brain firing in so many ways. I have heard that if you are unsure about what you want to do between two options, you should flip a coin. While it is in the air, since there is always one choice you want more than the other, your instincts will make the decision for you. You no longer even need to look at the coin. Suddenly, the solution to whatever you were wondering presents itself. *Voylah!*[8]

---

8 I like to intentionally mispronounce and misspell "voilà." Since y'all mispronounce "forte," this is my passive-aggressive grammar revenge.

But if that doesn't work, stop whatever you are doing, and go for a run. Or fiddle with a jigsaw puzzle. Or do anything that takes you out of the task you are trying to solve and makes you think in a different way. The vast majority of my good ideas[9] have come to me when I was out for a run. It is a proven that while running, you don't need a great deal of brainpower. Left, right, repeat is pretty simple. But the exercise is sending oxygen-rich blood coursing through your brain. Your brain then thanks you for the extra oxygen and puts it to good use with solutions, bursts of inspiration, and some far-out-there ideas. Buried in this metric ton of craziness, facts, song lyrics, and half-baked plans might just be the escape route out of the thinking slump you are in. This works for any sort of rhythmic exercise where you don't have to pay attention much. I wouldn't recommend it for cycling, however, as there are far too many outside-world factors that can make your life very unhappy if you aren't paying attention to them when you are cruising along at 25 miles per hour.

> *Make an empty space in any corner of your mind, and creativity will instantly fill it.*
> — Dee Hock

Other ways in which you can jump-start your brain seem rather obvious but mostly have to do with simply taking detours from our normal lives. Whether it is to paint a picture (even if you don't think you can paint), write a poem (even if you don't think your vocabulary is that strong), watch a movie outside of the genre you normally do, or call up a friend you haven't talked to in five years, all of these force you to break through habits that have been long ingrained in you. By point of survival, we are creatures of habit. Nothing is inherently wrong with that sort of behavior. But when we get

---

9 And, to be fair, many of my bad ideas.

stuck in a rut, we need to break those habits, if even just for a few minutes, to try to spark creativity.

Remember, you are not trying to be perfect when you are trying to think outside the hippo. The hippo isn't perfect.[10] What you are searching for are new ways to take on whatever is going on in your life. Granted, there will be few, if any, times where you are stuck with no answers and a random glance at a newspaper headline will solve your problems, like we see on TV all the time. But that's also not to say that exact scenario won't happen to you. You have to open yourself to new experiences in order to experience new things. You have to throw yourself into the cauldron of excitability[11] in order to be fully immersed by new ideas. Take a chance, as that's the only thing that will change your life. You have to look around for new ways to tackle the world if you want new ideas to come to you.

Remember, the Stone Age didn't end because they ran out of stones.

---

10   I mean, yeah, it is. Come on.
11   There's a fifty-fifty chance J. K. Rowling is going to say that the "cauldron of excitability" actually exists in Hogwarts somewhere.

CHAPTER 2
YOU DON'T HAVE TO; YOU GET TO

> *I am grateful for what I am and have.*
> *My thanksgiving is perpetual.*
> — Henry David Thoreau

How many times have you encountered a running friend who has said they *have* to run X miles today? Or a parent who says they *have* to take the kids to soccer practice? Or someone who has to do something that really isn't much of a "have to"? I readily admit I used to be one of those runners who felt it was a chore to be able to do something so awesome.[12]

To clarify, I use the past tense in describing myself as such not because I never experience the desire to sit on the couch and do nothing—quite the contrary. As much as I love exercise and feeling the wind whipping around me, I can unabashedly state that if liposuction were free, I would probably run less. There are days I just do not have the same desire to go for a run as I do on others. I will simply bide my time, dressed in my shoes and shorts, just hoping to get another spam email telling me that I need a better mortgage so I can delete it and shake my fist at the email gods and continue to not actu-

---

12 Obviously, this is not limited to the running world. I just use that example because it is one I hear the most often. You may have heard I run a bit.

ally go running. *Runcrastination*, I call it.[13]

But I know one thing for certain, and that is I do not *have* to run. No, dear sir or madam, as the case may be,[14] I *get* to run.

The distinct difference between "have to" and "get to" comes from the fact that all around us, there are people who would be glad to do the thing we are complaining about, but because of serious injuries or other circumstances, they have been robbed of that blessing. Allow me to use a personal anecdote here.

My own father was crippled in a hunting accident before I was born.[15] From the time I was cognizant until he passed away from Alzheimer's when I was thirty-four, I never so much as had a chance to play catch with him. He could get around for short distances with the use of a cane before exhaustion and pain took over and he had to sit down and rest. Therefore, obviously, running was not an option for him. I have no doubt, as much as he jokingly stated that my running feats were a bit on the outlandish side, he would have gladly joined me for one of those jaunts rather than continue to not have the choice to do so.

On a completely unrelated note, my father was once a three-pack-a-day smoker. Finally one day, the doctor told him to stop smoking or basically he would die. He ceased lighting up that same day and never smoked another cigarette the rest of his life. Many years later, I stated that this passage of time must have lessened his craving for cigarettes and asked him a question.

"You don't want them anymore, right?" I asked.

"Every single day," he said. Now that's intestinal fortitude.

Being without normal mobility, he lacked the choice to take his mind off his addiction by going for a run or taking up a similar hobby that would preoccupy the desire. Yet his wish to continue doing something, which even

---

13   *Procrunstination* just sounded painful.
14   Or both, if you are reading this together like one of those couples who sits on the same side of the booth at Applebee's. You aren't watching a movie, you two. Stop it.
15   I was born more than nine months after this accident, which means—if you can do the math—hats off to my dad.

the cigarette companies are finally admitting is almost criminally addictive, was always there. He fought against that desire because not doing so would have killed him. My father wasn't the best father in town—I wasn't the best son—yet some things he did amazed me. But I digress.

All around me I see similar circumstances where people who have lost limbs in war, have been devastated by disease, or have had something else awful befall them refuse to use those limitations as excuses for not going after what they want. Watching wheelchair racers in a marathon, or people using crutches in one of those obstacle course events, or mentally challenged individuals take years to earn a college degree, or anything else in between, is such an invigorating feeling. How can you possibly lament what you are able to do when you have that option to still do it?

Please note I am in no way saying you can't be upset about your lot in life. You can undoubtedly be unhappy with things that have or haven't happened. No one is particularly fond of being told, "Cheer up! It could be worse." My point being that when you dwell on what is so bad, you miss what is so good.

> *Reflect upon your present blessings—of which every man has many—not on your past misfortunes, of which all men have some.*
> — Charles Dickens

To reiterate, this is not to say our own sufferings and troubles need to always be compared to others who have it worse. We are welcome to have our own down moments and lulls of appreciation as to the gifts we have. It truly is difficult to always be thankful of what we have, but that doesn't mean we shouldn't at least try to be so. Gratitude is something that needs to be tended to each day.

The easiest way to do so is to give yourself a thank-you. Thank yourself for making the right choices on what you ate that day. Give yourself a bit of praise for deciding to take the stairs instead of the elevator. Allow yourself a small pat on the back for going to bed on time. These small bits of self-gratitude will then filter out into the world. If others see you are rewarding yourself for good decisions, they, too, will try to do the same. Nothing wrong with a bunch of people doing good things and then being happy that they did them!

While you shouldn't focus too much on what others do or do not have, if you are having a little bit of difficulty in seeing the good in your own life, do take a broad look around. Do you have a roof over your head? Running water? A warm meal? Well, if so, then you have it better than a wide swath of the entire world. You don't have to go that deep or that dark to look for those who are worse off than you, but it never hurts to do a quick count of the simplest of your fortunes.

Now expand it a little bit more. Think about that workout you *have* to do, or the book you *have* to write, or the children you *have* to take to whatever recital, practice, and so forth. Then realize how lucky you are that you *get* to do those things.

I was talking to a person once who lost complete use of their legs. Wheelchair bound, they were filled with effervescence, always smiling and happy. Trying to understand how they could be so happy when they no longer had use of their legs, I asked them almost point blank how that was possible.

"I don't know how so many people who can walk are so miserable" was their answer.

This struck me like a wave. Indeed, how (outside of actual depression and mental health issues), when you have the ability of complete and free locomotion, could you ever truly be in a bad mood over trivial things? Of course bills are due. Yes, that guy cut you off in traffic. But when you assess every single thing in this world that you have the complete luxury to do and are not doing, it is a bit shameful.

> *You will never find time for anything.*
> *If you want time you must make it.*
> — Charles Buxton

There is only one thing you absolutely have to do on this planet: die. You don't have to pay bills. You don't have to eat. You don't have to do anything whatsoever. There will be consequences, but you aren't absolutely forced to do those things. The complete list of what is certain in your life is that it will end. Everything else falls into the other category of what you get to choose to do—the "get to" category. So if you want to, and you aren't, you have to ask yourself why not.

Then go do it.

CHAPTER 3
ACCEPT YOUR TALENT

While reading an interview for an otherworldly talented athlete, I saw them mention something akin to "I have worked extremely hard. I was not blessed with talent or good genes." Who the athlete was is not important. I have actually seen this same statement time and time again by supremely talented athletes and gifted intellectuals in every field you can imagine over the years. In fact, famed runner Steve Prefontaine once said, "Hell, there are a dozen other guys on the team with more talent in their little finger than I've got."

Steve Prefontaine. The guy with one of the highest recorded VO2 maxes in history.[16]

Look, I get why they say it. Mainly, they don't want to let the fact that something they have no control over (predetermined DNA) take precedence over that which they do (work hard). To a great extent, they are correct in the idea that hard work matters. You can have all the talent in the world, but if you never utilize it, it is useless. As such, the thinking is, *Sure, I have good genes, but I am still busting my butt.* Indeed, if you are at the top level

---

16 You may have heard this term, but it basically means the measurement of the maximum amount of oxygen a person can utilize during intense exercise. The higher the max, the longer you can exercise before muscle fatigue sets in. For many of us, that max is reached when we hear our dog in the other room eating something he shouldn't and we have to run into make sure it isn't chocolate.

of your sport, or game, or business, you got there because you worked hard. Why isn't talent alone enough to give you success at the top levels? Because all the other people at the top are talented too. To differentiate yourself, you must give something else. You rose through the normal ranks of the rest of us riffraff, even quite possibly doing so with less than a great deal of effort, because you were genetically superior to us. There isn't a single thing wrong with that. But then when things get tougher, it is those with a better work ethic who are the pinnacle of success. But you still had that DNA to start the game off with.

> *The man who has confidence in himself*
> *gains the confidence of others.*
> — Hasidic saying

When I speak about *ignoring the impossible*, I go against the grain of many who like to try to motivate and inspire. I hesitated for years even thinking about writing a motivational book because I am not a cheerleader. I am not one who says you can do anything you want. That everything is possible. That with the right amount of effort, you can solve any problem. Am I a negative person? No. I am realist. There are plenty of things you cannot and will not ever be able to accomplish. But trying is not one of them.

I mention that you are not necessarily able to do everything you put your mind to because I want people to focus on reality. There are just some things you will never achieve. Taken the wrong way, some may use what I have just said as an excuse to never try at all. If they can't do it because their genes forbid it, then why even attempt? The reason is simple: because you never know what you can do unless you try. Then try again. And keep trying.

In *The Empire Strikes Back*, Yoda famously said: "Do or do not. There is no try." Well, Yoda was a puppet, and George Lucas wrote horrible prequels that didn't completely tank only because so many of us Gen Xers absolutely loved the previous stories he seemingly lucked into creating.[17] Yoda wasn't a prophet. Trying is the most important thing in the world. In fact, it is the only thing you can do. What happens afterward is only a result of you trying. Case in point: I failed miserably in my first marathon. I then went and built a career based on what I achieved in the running world after that fact. Trying was 100 percent how that happened.

But this success didn't come easily. It also didn't come quickly. In addition, success has never been constant for me either. I have had ups and downs even after thinking I was done having ups and downs. I mean, what more can a person do after running fifty-two marathons in fifty-two weekends to try to show you what is possible? Apparently, more is still needed. So it took me years of continually rebuilding myself, upping the ante, and challenging my body in ways I never thought possible before I was finally what I considered a success. (In hindsight, I realize how ridiculous that whole mind-set was, but I will get to that later.)

In the interim, there were years where I was almost flat broke, borrowing money from family members and taking out loans, all the while hearing close friends ask me why I just didn't take my law degree and get a job. Here I was, in their mind, sitting on a goldmine of wealth if I just took my doctorate and did an honest day's work. But they didn't understand that I never wanted a job. I wanted, at least in their parlance, a career. Ideally, I wanted to make money doing something that I completely controlled while also hopefully helping people along the way. In doing so, I realized that not everyone can do everything.

At the same time, I realized it was completely illogical to not accept that some people are simply more talented than we are in certain aspects. That is how the world works. To deny you had some help from the DNA fairy (or God, or whatever you believe) is the epitome of arrogance. It is also a slight to those who do not achieve greatness. "Well, maybe you need to work harder." This whole line of thinking is what I find wrong about books that

---

17 Take that, billionaire. I hope he survives this scathing takedown.

preach there is a secret to controlling your destiny. If the chips fall where you want them to, according to their line of thought, it is because you worked hard or thought the right way. If they don't, it is because you need to work harder or put those feelings out into the universe in a different manner.

No.

Sometimes you just aren't going to be able to dunk a basketball. So learn how to shoot better. If you can't shoot better, play another sport. Being bad at something is not a problem. Pretending that everyone can be good at something *is* the problem. In addition, acting as if you aren't good at something at which you are clearly proficient is an insult to those who aren't and desperately would do anything to have that gift.

So simply accept it. Yes, you rise early in the morning to grind. Sure, you have four kids or came from poverty. Absolutely, your drive and determination are to be envied. But when the cards were dealt, you got a nice hand to start with. There is nothing wrong with that.

However, no matter how well you started, if you don't play those cards correctly, you will end up losing your shirt. So why should you put your talents into action? Let me break that down for you.

THEY CAN BE LUCRATIVE

I am not saying money is the most important thing in the world.[18] But money allows us to do everything else in the world, which includes all the good and wonderful things. So start there. Don't feel guilty that you want to make your life more comfortable by utilizing what you have. Don't feel bad knowing society has created a system where funny colored paper can be exchanged for the food you wish to give to the hungry, or the seeds to plant the woods that give us the trees to build houses for the homeless, or

---

18   But you can't buy tacos with a good attitude, so I am not *not* saying it isn't either.

the medicine for the sick, or the books for those who wish to learn. That's our system. Work it.

Your talents can be utilized in such ways to make your life simpler, which allows you to do the same for others. Only when you are in a position of at least a little bit of comfort can you think outside yourself to make the situations better for people who *aren't* you. Once you get to that point, then your talents can improve everyone else's situations.

THE BENEFITS OF OUR TALENTS EXTEND TO OTHERS

No one is useless in this world who lightens the burdens of another.
— Charles Dickens

We have all gotten to where we are because of someone else. In Malcolm Gladwell's book *Outliers: The Story of Success*, Gladwell writes about Bill Gates and his success with Microsoft. Absolutely, Bill was successful because of his intellect and his ruthless ambition, but he also succeeded because of luck and circumstances. Gates attended a high school with a fellow student who happened to have a mom who founded a firm called C-Cubed at the University of Washington. After school, Gates worked at the C-Cubed offices and programmed long into the evening on one of the only computers in the nation that could do what he needed it to do at that time.

Later down the road, Gates began working for a company that agreed to let him have free computer time in exchange for working on a particular piece of software. By the sheer luck of living in the right place at the right time, Gates was able to utilize his talents. If Gates had lived in Paducah, Kentucky,[19] where no such computer existed, chances are we would not have

---

19   My favorite name for a place on planet Earth.

Microsoft. Microsoft absolutely changed the way life works for every single one of us today. That only happened because of the people who surrounded one of the more gifted people of our lifetime. The talents of others laid the groundwork for the programming computers Gates would use to hone his skills; they didn't even know they were helping create the richest man in the world. But their existence helped change modern computing into what it is today.

YOU CAN CHANGE LIVES

> *You have not lived today until you have done something*
> *for someone who can never repay you.*
> — John Bunyan

While you must not necessarily seek out those who are so destitute they can't repay you, or give anonymously so that is it impossible for someone to thank you for your efforts, the axiom above rings true nonetheless. Our marks are left on the world by those who continue to remember us, or our actions, long after we pass. Accumulating wealth alone without attempting to help others rarely leaves any sort of a good legacy.

Instead, look to lend a hand or a lift a spirit whenever you can. I often read stories about artists or athletes who made the days of a few fans simply by signing autographs. I think how wonderful it must be to know that by just scribbling your name on a napkin, you may completely change the existence of someone who admires you. That's all they need to do. A pat on the back, a hello and a smile, or something small will mean the world to someone who looks up to you. People who admire you often only need a nugget of your time or compassion in order to be so fulfilled. If you have it to give, you should.

We may even change someone's life just because we exercise our gifts. It doesn't need to be a huge expenditure on your part. Start small and do something. Pick up some litter. Plant a tree. Hold the door for someone as you walk into the grocery store. Someone out there someday will be inspired because of what you did, and if they aren't, you still did something good. As Gandhi once said, "When you do things right, people won't be sure you've done anything at all."[20]

Having been on both sides of this equation, even on the minutest of levels, I can tell you it warms your soul to do something that a fan or follower appreciates. Once, a reader said her young daughter was a fan, so I sent her a signed picture of myself. It was the first piece of actual real mail this young girl had ever received in today's electronic age. She loved the fact that mail came addressed to her so much that she even kept the envelope!

YOUR TALENTS CAN PUT YOU ON THE PATH TO A MORE GRATIFYING EXISTENCE

Extensive research has been conducted on people who attempt to utilize their strengths and how it affects their overall quality of life. Unsurprisingly, people who apply that which comes naturally are almost ten times more likely to be engaged with their occupations.

Doing so improved their health and wellness, which provided them with more energy to focus on the task at hand. In addition, while we should definitely strive to improve our weaknesses, studies have also shown that doing so at the detriment of making use of your strengths is a bad idea.

As a personal example, while I have occasionally competed in triathlons, I am limited by my travel schedule to how often I ride my bike. One might think that I should really focus on improving that portion to become a better triathlete. But what I have found while experimenting with the best way to

---

20   I'm kidding. This is from *Futurama*.

improve is that when I focus more on the bike and let the other two disciplines slack off, my overall times go down. Ideally, I could both increase my time on the bike and keep my talents the same on the other two disciplines. However, when faced with a time crunch, I continue to hone my skills at running and swimming and use the athleticism I have created there to make up for the lack of time spent in the saddle. In the end, by focusing on what I am already good at, I end up enjoying myself more, and my times are actually better at the finish.

It doesn't take a genius to see how much more rewarding your day-to-day life can be when you are doing something you not only enjoy, but at which you excel. Of course, you are still putting in the time, and it is work, and yes you might be on a deadline, but if you are spending your efforts on something that makes the best use of the skills you have, your life in general is going to be better.

We all have talents, skills, and passions. Find out what yours are, and do something with them!

CHAPTER 4
KNOW YOUR WORTH

> *The greatest danger for most of us is not that our aim is too high and we miss it, but that it is too low and we reach it.*
> — Michelangelo[21]

How you conduct business determines how successful you will be. This seems like an obvious statement, but there are so many obvious things that still need to be said. Allow me to share with you a conversation I once had over email with someone.[22]

Person: Hey, Dane, since you do what you do, how about the chance to do it for me, for free, on my website so I can draw attention to my website/races/magazine. Here is a link with the details! (*Link shows I would pay my own way to races, run them, and report back to Person my thoughts and feelings on the race.*)

Me: Thanks, Person. But I see no benefit for me in doing this.

---

21   Not the Teenage Mutant Ninja Turtle.
22   I am paraphrasing only to be vague about the person and not call undue attention to their inanity. But they know who they are. They know.

Person: Really? Why?

Me: Perhaps you can explain to me the benefit.

Person: Well, you run a lot of races, and it would be cool to know what races (you have either fun [*sic*] of [*sic*] want to run) you think are the best. That's all.[23]

Me: Well, of course it would benefit people to have my take on the races. But, as I said, I don't see the benefit to *me* to do all that work and share it for no compensation. You know I am writing a book of must-run races right now, right?

Person: Just forget Dane [*sic*]. Good luck to you!

Me: By all means if I am missing something, please convey it to me.

(*No response.*)

I guarantee you, this person feels I missed out on this opportunity to be an ambassador or whatever name he wanted to give to the free labor he was hoping I would provide. Part of the problem with doing some relatively intangible line of work (e.g., speaking or writing) is that people think nothing of asking you to do it for free or for "exposure." This is one of the many reasons why this whole idea of doing things to be seen without compensation is a bunch of hooey.[24] Granted, there are people in every line of work who are hungry for any sort of attention. Giving them the pleasure of seeing their name next to a byline in a magazine when they are simply a blogger is hard to pass up. Throw in some socks, too, or maybe even some branded

---

23   Direct quote. If it took you a while to figure that out, congrats—you like English to be written coherently!

24   *Hooey* is a very smart business term.

swag so they can say they have a sponsorship deal, and good luck getting that person to shut up about *X* brand.

Believe me, I comprehend how smart a move this is for businesses today. They have created a culture where *seeming* important is somehow sought after more so than actually *being* important. Being famous for being famous is an extremely lucrative venture for a handful of people. But it is highly unlikely that you are that person.

> *Find out what you like doing best, and get*
> *someone to pay you for doing it.*
> — Katherine Whitehorn

Through a decade of hard work and achievements, I have created a brand that means something. I might not be a Kardashian,[25] and some might not see the value in what I have created. But I have said many times, to many people, the greatest strength comes in knowing your worth. Sure, you question that value when someone of fairly decent status in your field sends you the messages above. But when you know the reason they reached out to you in the first place is because they themselves see value in what you do, you have to trust you know what you are doing.

Even if your relative value is not as great as another's, you must trust that what you have created does have worth. Do not give it away for free. Don't write for *HuffPost* for nothing. Don't do TED Talks out of the kindness of your heart. You have to realize both these organizations, and many more, charge tons of money for tickets and subscriptions. Why shouldn't you receive payment for the work that is the backbone of what they do? In a world where people share Netflix passwords and Costco cards, make people pay you what you are worth.

---

25   Thank all that is good and holy.

How do you find out your value? As mentioned above, if people are asking for your help on an issue, then right away, you realize that someone thinks you can help them. If you are already in a field—not even as an expert but as someone with a little bit of knowledge—you have done hard work to get there. People are coming to you to solve a problem or find a solution because of the work you have done. That has value. Charge for it.

People are going to want to "pick your brain." Decline said offer. Tell them that you have a fee structure that you would be happy to provide for them as a consultant. Undoubtedly some will proffer, "How about I grab some lunch and ask you some questions?" Now they not only want your mind, but they want your time. And for what? A ham sandwich? You are a good person. You obviously want to help. But you also need to make sure that you are being compensated. Give them a quote. If they balk at the price, you didn't lose a potential customer. They had no intention of paying you anyway.

I learned this the hard way once when I was asked to consult on putting on a race. I met for lunch, had it paid for, and was presented with an idea. I thought I did the right thing by presenting a quote. I was met with many reassurances. As I am a "get things done" type of person, I got to getting things done. In a week alone, I put more hours into this project than most people do in a month to get this sort of race off the ground. Then the other shoe dropped. I realized that all promises of sponsors and race registrations (which my fee was contingent upon) were fabricated. Well, I didn't learn they were fabricated until weeks later. I thought, at the time, they were merely exaggerated or there was a misunderstanding. But I continued to do work under the sunk cost fallacy.

If you don't know what the sunk cost fallacy is, I guarantee you have done it. A sunk cost is a cost that has already occurred and cannot be recovered by any means. The fallacy comes when you continue to throw bad money and time after good. In other words, you stick with a decision because you have already put effort into it and you want to see it through, even when you are almost assured the end result will be undesirable. Well, fortunately, even though I fell prey to this fallacy for a few weeks more, I finally cut ties with the person. I still held all the pertinent info for putting on the race and, despite begging and pleading from the person who needed it, never gave it to them.[26]

This felt awful to do because I like to think I am a reasonable chap. But it was the only thing I had of value left. If they wanted it, they had to justly compensate me for it. Either way, I wiped my hands of the project before it got deeper.

Learn from my example. Trust your gut. If you feel like someone isn't going to compensate you for your time and expertise, chances are you are right. Simply asking them to do so will prove it one way or another.

> *A person's worth in this world is estimated*
> *according to the value they put on themselves.*
> — Jean de La Bruyère

If you still wish to throw a few tidbits of info to someone because he is your brother-in-law or your kids play on the same soccer team, keep it general. Give the why and what but never the how. Don't even point them in the direction to obtain the how. That's shortchanging yourself.

You can always exchange for equal value as well. This puts you in an advantageous bargaining position. In my example above, I knew I was never going to get back for my time and work, but I held the only bargaining chip. If they wanted it in order to move forward, I had to at least get something from them. This something might not be money, but if you can assess what they have that can be of equal benefit for you, you may be able come to an agreement eventually. Just stick to it this time, and get it up front.

---

26 Literal quote in an email: "Are you going to give me access to all that you created? It didn't cost you anything."

Don't back down. This is key. When the person in my initial example about writing for his website told me to forget it, I was bummed. I respected this person. I thought maybe we could come to a compromise. But ignoring my next reply told me everything I needed to know. They wanted something (and a lot of it) for nothing. Most people are afraid to draw a line in the sand as they fear they may anger a friend or lose a potential client or opportunity. However, if someone will walk away because you won't freely dispense advice, they weren't much of a friend or weren't going to pay you anyway. You are better off without them.

You see, when you know your worth, no one can disrespect you. You will have the strength and the courage to remove yourself from situations that do not benefit you. Instead of overcoming hurdles that are in the way, you will instead refuse to go the way of most resistance and save yourself the trouble in the first place. Why leap when you can simply sidestep?

Save your energy for sex. It's far healthier anyway.

CHAPTER 5
DO IT FOR YOU

I am only putting one quote in this book that I vehemently disagree with:

> *The greatest pleasure in life is doing what*
> *people say you cannot do.*
> — Walter Bagehot

Let me be crystal clear: those who say you can't are *not* an inspiration. Do not use people who only try to stop you from achieving your goals for no reason other than to be contrary as the ones who fuel your desire to do anything. No matter what you do, you will not turn naysayers into yaysayers.[27]

I see this defiant attitude all the time. It boils down to a "You said I couldn't; now watch me while I do" stance, which I find to be counterproductive to a happy mind-set. There are few worse ways to live your life than to derive pleasure from accomplishing what others say you can or cannot do.

27　This is by far the fruitiest, most bumper-sticker slogan I will probably have in this book, but it couldn't be truer.

Achieving whatever you think is success or fulfillment should not be either spurred on, or validated, by negative opinions. Perhaps the reason some feel this mind-set has merit stems from the fact that studies show negative people are seen as being more intelligent. So the thinking goes, if you can prove those people wrong, they are not as smart as they think they are. You have not only one-upped them by showing them what you can do but have knocked them down a peg or two.

Obviously, there is a certain amount of comeuppance; we enjoy giving the business to those who stand in our way. I mean, I understand why it can feel good to stick it to someone. Making it the crux of your enjoyment is a horrible idea and will not give you happiness for long. You see, there are many things in life that feel better than showing people they were wrong. Indeed, not caring at all what people say about your wants and dreams might just be the best feeling in the world. Indifference is freeing. It is the opposite of hatred. It is like removing a cloud over your head, a weight off your shoulders and allows you to float above the junk below you.

Is it easy not to care about what people say? Of course not. No one who is a decent person likes to have people put down their desires. Even those in the public eye who have to develop thicker skins don't like to hear negativity spewed from the anonymous (or not-so-anonymous) reaches of the internet. But focusing your mind on the task at hand and ignoring those who say nay is the best use of your time and energy. Then, when you do what was deemed impossible, celebrate with the ones who supported you rather than giving the jerks who derided you more attention. Why take away good vibes from people who like you so you can waste time on those who don't?

Let me take a moment to drive this point home. We see the "Nobody believed in us!" attitude prevalent in sports teams now. Even multiple-championship-winning teams, chock-full of superstars, develop this "us against the world" mentality. But think about when you want to "prove everybody wrong" about whom *everybody* encompasses. Of course it includes the few jerks that are the ire and reason behind your stance. But it also covers the people who don't know you but might support you if they did. More importantly, it lumps into this group all the people who are 100 percent behind you. Your family. Your close friends. People who are happy to see you do well. Yet instead of thanking them for the times they drove you to soccer practice, or gave you that loan to start your own board game, or allowed you to crash on their couch when you were overcoming addiction and had no place to go, you are now spending more time and energy on the people who will never care if you succeed. How preposterous is that mind-set? How much of a waste of time and energy on your part is it to give those people another thought? Think about how much of an insult it is to those who have lent you their ears, their shoulders, or anything else to get you to where you are.

Instead, know that virtually everything difficult achieved by anyone throughout history was seen as impossible or ludicrous by many. If you truly wish to accomplish something and feel the best at having done it, the only way you can achieve that is by doing it for yourself. The satisfaction of completing what you hoped you could do is a delicious treat that should be savored by you and those who care about you.

OK, I am going to just accept that some of you aren't totally on board with this way of viewing the world. There is still a bit of reverse schaden-freude we can get from doing something good to prove people wrong. So instead of using actual people and allowing those people to have some control over your emotions, invent a Ron Summer.

What's a Ron Summer? Well, it is a generic name I created many years ago to embody all the terrible things people may say about me or think about me or wish upon me. I imbue Ron, as a stand-in for awful people, with all sorts of negative attributes. He is jealous and petty. He is a busybody. He tries to think that what he is doing is for the betterment of society when all it really is about is to fulfill his only need for self-love. Heck, he's even got a horrible comb-over, and his mouth is filled with bad teeth. Basically, he is like a troll from *The Lord of the Rings*. I try to make him as physically and mentally repulsive as possible. Then, instead of worrying about what people might say or do to stop me from achieving my goals, I lump every one of those people into one: Ron Summer.

Ron is the one who wants me to fail. Ron is the one who hopes that even my successes are tinged with caveats. Even if I do complete a task or achieve a goal, Ron will never be happy. No amount of me doing good will ever be enough for Ron. Then a funny thing happens. I no longer wish to try to please Ron. Instead, I really begin to feel sorry for him.

Here is a person who wakes up every day wanting me to do nothing but fail. I hardly ever think of Ron, but not a second goes by where Ron isn't infuriated by me. Everything I do brings him discomfort and unhappiness. I occupy his thoughts, his emails, and his Google searches. Now the sorrow turns to pity. I can't possibly care about pleasing this type of person because he will never be happy with anything.

I wish he could see the world differently. Instead of trying to find negative everywhere, he should look for positive things to affirm his happiness. I feel sorry for Ron. But he is a blech-filled clay person who doesn't have the capacity for rational thought or kindness. So, instead of wanting to prove Ron wrong, I just end up hoping that what I do will inspire Ron to become a better person himself. Maybe, like Pinocchio, he can become a real boy. Now I no longer spend a single second thinking about Ron.

> *A successful man is one who can lay a firm foundation*
> *with the bricks others have thrown at him.*
> — David Brinkley

By following my lead on this, you can take away any negative power from those who try to stop you and put it on your own version of Ron. Because I feel nothing but sorrow for the way Ron chooses to his live his life, I am now only doing what I do for myself and those who matter to me. I have completely robbed Ron (and therefore anyone else like him who wishes me ill) of any power whatsoever.

I can better appreciate what I want to do without wondering whether someone else will think positively about it. Sharing my good moments with those who care that I do well makes so much more sense. I wonder how I ever would have worried about those who want nothing but bad for me. Suddenly, wanting to do something to prove anyone else wrong is the furthest thing from my mind. Now that my own victories taste sweeter, I can fully cherish the flavor of my successes without the spiteful aftertaste of needing to prove others wrong.

And it tastes really good.

CHAPTER 6
"THEIR LIFE HELPED"

I once read a story where someone was asked about a recently deceased friend. The person, at an evident loss for words on how to adequately sum up all that their friend meant to them, finally settled on this simple maxim: "Their life helped." Frankly, I can think of no greater compliment, and I hope that this is written on my tombstone.

Mattering to yourself is important. The bonus of mattering to people is that it makes your own experience on earth that much more fulfilling. When you have a value that is beyond your own worth, you can often fall back on that in your own times of trouble. Can't quite break through on a project you are trying to create? Maybe help someone else on theirs. Recently gone through a heartbreak? Undoubtedly someone else has as well, and your experience might offer a fresh perspective for them. If others rely on you, or need you, or want you around, you have increased your own worth a thousandfold. When you help others, they are more likely to also help people. You can easily see how this becomes the greatest pyramid scheme of all time. Each person helping others until everyone is taken care of all the way down the line.

But how do you get to a point where your life can "help," so to speak? Well, the simple fact of the matter is that in order to improve the lives of others, the first thing you must do is look at yourself from another person's point of view.

Do you like how you're seen by others? If not, perhaps there are things you can change that will present yourself in a better light. But more than likely, you are being too harsh on yourself. If you have friends,[28] look at how they view you. They probably see your value in places you haven't even considered. If you gauge yourself as others do and see what you add to the equation of the human race, you have already begun the process of changing bad things to good. The first domino to topple to make the entire world better is to value yourself first.

With a clearer understanding of what you have to offer, you can become a better tool for helping others. Obviously the goal is not to change every aspect of yourself and become someone you are not. Rather, one should strive to support friends in need. Maybe you know someone who needs a shoulder to cry on. Perhaps they desperately require a small loan until they get their next paycheck. Or maybe all they desire is to bounce some ideas off you for their next work assignment. Listening and being present are the absolute best gifts you can give to anyone. Your time is finite. When you share some of it with someone, you are sharing the most precious resource you have.

> *Those who are happiest are those who do the most for others.*
> — Booker T. Washington

When you decide to share your time with them, don't waste that opportunity. Put your phone down. Stop watching TV. Be in the now. Let them see your eyes the entire time they are speaking to you. Don't just hear them; take their words into your heart. Do not simply wait until they are done speaking to offer some rote advice. Listen. Listen so intently that when they do finish speaking, you might even need a few seconds to form a sentence.

---

28   I have six.

Not because you weren't paying attention but rather because you were in the moment so much you weren't trying to solve the problem. You were just there.

Now tell them that. Tell them you are quiet because you want to know if they want to talk more. Ask them if they want you to simply let them sound off or if they want you to help them brainstorm. Make it clear that you are there for them.

Just be ready.

SMILE AT SOMEONE—ANYONE

Helping the world and yourself doesn't just come from large gestures and energies like giving your precious time. You can improve the world with roughly ten muscles—the ones that make you smile. Contrary to popular adages, it takes maybe a few more muscles to smile than it does to frown. So smiling is actually better for you simply because it works out your face more. So do it. Liberally.

If someone makes eye contact with you, smile. If someone serves you, smile. If someone opens a door for you, hands you a napkin, or just makes your heart happy to be around them—smile! You have the power to turn someone's entire day around by simply smiling. It is an extremely inexpensive currency that you never run out of and never depreciates.

> *Show me a smile, and I'll show you one back.*
> — Vanilla Ice[29]

---

29   Yep. Vanilla, Robert Matthew Van Winkle, Ice.

A friend of mine was in a complicated relationship once. A misunderstanding was mixed in with confusion, which only obfuscated the truth. They were at loggerheads with their partner. Suddenly it became clear to the other person that all the bad feelings were predicated on simple confusion. Heartache that had been building for weeks and the feeling that everything was crumbling around them suddenly was gone. Their partner just smiled. They smiled deep. They smiled hard.

While my friend didn't know if all their problems were fixed, that smile changed the entire mood of the moment. The room lit up, a dreary mood and cloudiness of soul parted, and it was clear that something was changing. When you see the sparkle in the eye of a loved one, it is impossible to be in a bad mood. This smile facilitated a long discussion that made everything so much clearer. Feelings poured out. Tears soon followed. Suddenly there were laughter and wet eyes. All because of one little smile.

COMPLIMENT AND MEAN IT

Often people are afraid to give compliments because they wonder how the other person will take it. But if you mean what you say, then you should never hesitate to tell someone else. You have no idea what a simple kind word can do to turn around the day of another. When you truly believe what you have to say, people can tell.

Don't have an agenda when you pay a compliment. Like smiling, be plentiful with your compliments. Compliment people of all sexes and genders. Compliment older people. Younger people. Everyone. If someone makes you happy or you like what they are doing, be direct. Don't try to make a flirtatious comment. Simply say, "Love the way you do that thing you do, Steve."[30]

---

30   n.b. I have almost never liked what Steve has done, and he knows it. (Fingers from my eyes to his.)

Send a note to a doctor who helped you through a rough time. Send a note to a college professor who made you see the world in a different way. Send a note to someone who did something thoughtful, not because it was expected, but simply because they could.

Expected compliments feel good. Unexpected compliments have a huge and lasting impact.

If you send the compliment in writing, that note may be displayed for a long time. It may serve as a reminder that every job, no matter how seemingly thankless or invisible, is appreciated by at least one person: you. And that's an awesome way to be remembered.

Also, *accept* compliments. The thing about how other people feel that is important for you to remember is that it really doesn't matter if you feel the same way. If they like your hair, it doesn't matter if you think you are having a bad hair day. If they think you are wonderful for how you listen to their stories, but you feel it is just what people should do, well, they obviously think it is noteworthy. Just say, "Thank you." That's all you have to do. No hemming and hawing. No equivocating. No self-deprecation. Just say thank you.

APOLOGIZE TO A PERSON YOU LET DOWN

If there is a rival to the words "I love you" when it comes to saying the absolute most to someone, it might be "I am sorry." We all make mistakes. Sometimes they are doozies. We do things we regret, or we omit things we should do. Every one of us has failed to step up when we should have, to have shown support that was needed, or to have been there for those who matter. We can't control some of the errors we have made. But we can control how we act afterward.

Chances are high whatever the mistake was, you have moved past it. Chances are also high the other person hasn't. A situation might be at least partially forgotten because someone who was harmed knows they have done the same thing to others in the past, maybe even to you. But simply admitting you are wrong and expressing sorrow that it happened can mean the difference between a relationship ending and one that grows stronger.

> *It's incredible how many wounds can be*
> *healed by the two words "I'm sorry."*
> — Matshona Dhliwayo

There is no statute of limitation on an apology either. In fact, the longer the passage of time, the stronger an affect an apology can have. Blurting out an "I'm sorry!" seconds after a transgression can often be seen as trite and done to only placate someone who was harmed. On the contrary, by letting what has happened totally soak in, and when the heat of the moment has passed, having the gumption to own up to what you have done will slay the elephant in the room more times than not.

Make sure the apology is pure too. No disclaimers. No "but" in the middle. It is likely you were wronged as well. It is likely the other person knows this. Just handle your own apology, and make sure they know you are taking your part of the blame. No matter what happens, you control how you react to any situation. Letting someone know you want to make whatever went wrong into something better is all you should care about.

This apology might not fix everything immediately, and it might not fix anything ever. The point of the apology is not about making everything right. It is about letting someone know that you wish it was fixed, and this is what you are doing to start that process.

EXPRESS YOUR CONGRATULATIONS

Akin to smiling at a stranger, sharing congratulations can even be done to people you don't know. As an author, I can't tell how you a simple "Wow, I really liked your book!" from someone I have never met has completely changed my mood. Like most authors, I write in a vacuum,[31] send it to editors, get it printed, and take it to book signings. Most of the interactions I have with people are usually before they read the book. Getting a thumbs-up from a reader is a gold mine of happiness.

Granted, social media helps us do this with relative strangers, but just because it is easier doesn't mean you shouldn't do it. If someone loses weight—tell them congrats. If you see them sell a house as a Realtor—let them know they did a good job. Promotion at that job they love? Yaybeans! Finished a small task that makes them happy? Share in the joy! It is truly so easy that we shouldn't ever stop telling people congrats for all the things that go on daily.

But for the love of Zeus, do not say "Congrats! I was wondering if you could help me with…" or "That's awesome! Let me tell you about how I also did something." Keep your wishes directed toward the person for two seconds. Don't make it about you. The only time you should bring yourself into the equation is when you are telling the person how their accomplishment had a positive impact on you personally. Let them know that because of what they have done, you were motivated to do that task you had been putting off forever. Tell them they became an inspiration to you and helped you see things differently. By doing so, you have made your congratulations personal. Now you are not only telling them that they did a good job but also showing them the positive real-world repercussions of their actions.

---

31   It's a Dyson, so it is at least really expensive and roomy.

MAKE A SINCERE OFFER OF HELP

As most people see the act of asking for help as a major sign of weakness, they are more than likely not going to go through with actually seeking assistance. Doing so leaves them vulnerable and open to rejection and also admits they cannot do everything on their own.

Yet everyone needs help. I learned long ago it is not *what* you know in this world but *whom* you know. This is difficult to subscribe to when you think you can conquer anything with just enough initiative and desire. But we need others, and we need them to guide us. So since that is the case, take the hippo by the oxpecker,[32] and ask someone if they need your assistance. What they need may be something you are unable to provide, but don't let it be from a lack of trying. Furthermore, be specific when you are seeking to help. A general question like "Do you need any help?" is more than likely to be met with the reply of "No, I'm good." Well, Karen, you aren't good, and I can tell. That's why I am asking.

Approach the situation, and say something akin to "Hey, I have worked on something like this and found that I made so many errors before I found out what to do. If you are stuck, let's brainstorm." Or, even if you know more about the situation, ask them how they are going about tackling the problem. This will be an opportunity for them to show you what they know, and you can take it from there. If you don't have expertise, suggest finding someone together who does. Two people asking for help is no longer a weakness. In fact, showing that finding a solution was tough for two people will put your friend at ease and make the one who figures out the solution feel super-duper special.

By sharing the load of figuring out the problem, you have now invested yourself in the solution to make sure the other person is not alone. You are now in the situation together.

---

32 You knew that one was coming.

> *There are so many people in the world with so little. Who cares why you decide to help?*
> — Amy Poehler

BELIEVE IN SOMEONE'S DREAMS

You can be both pragmatic and also allow your head to swim in the clouds. It takes nothing whatsoever to tell someone that you believe in them. That you believe in their dreams. That you can see that what they want is important to them and if hoping alone can make it happen, then you have more than enough of that to bring it all to fruition. This costs absolutely nothing. Just a positive attitude and an outlook that says, "I am here for you, and I want you to go get what you want." The power that comes from simply looking someone in the eye and, with conviction and honesty, letting them know you believe in them is almost limitless.

When you have this belief, it will undoubtedly be returned. When you support those you care about and help lift them up, they will bring you with them when they rise. If the time comes when you need a little help, someone you assisted is far more likely to support you than someone you didn't. Not that getting something in return should be the impetus for helping, but it isn't a bad incentive. By jumping in with both feet and splashing away in the river of their dreams, you will more likely get soaked with their assistance later on.[33]

A rising tide raises all boats, as they say.

---

33   That was a ridiculously wet metaphor, but I liked it anyway.

SAY THANK YOU TO THOSE WHO BELIEVED IN YOU

Some people have a never-ending well of self-belief. But most people have tons of doubts and are lent confidence and self-assurance by others. That's why those who believe in us are the backbone of what we become. Because of their encouragement and support, we develop a stronger sense of self.

Yet even those who never seem to doubt themselves will, at some time, need others to believe in them. They got to where they are by being buttressed by others. That is why they are there for you now. Someone looked past your own self-doubt and witnessed in you something you didn't see yourself. As much as we would like to think we are all self-made, you are where you are because others helped you. So thank those people.

> *Showing gratitude is one of the simplest yet most powerful things humans can do for each other.*
> — Randy Pausch

Sit people down, and tell them how much their sacrifice and time has meant to you. Let them know that without their beliefs, things would be different in your life. Acknowledge all they have done for you, and you will assuredly be paying them back for what they have given to you. We have all heard of a vicious cycle. This is the most wonderful cycle possible.[34]

---

34   Other than the light cycles from *TRON*. Those are just so cool.

CHAPTER 7
BE AFRAID

OK, that was an attention-grabbing chapter title. You really shouldn't be afraid, per se.[35] But if you are nervous or excited or anxious or any of those other emotions before the start of your race or your big speech in front of your coworkers or before you propose to your hopefully soon-to-be-spouse, that is a fantastic feeling to have, and you should embrace it. Let me explain why.

When I am doing my usual routine of book signing and answering eighteen quazillion questions at a race expo, I can almost immediately identify many of the first-time runners. They are more or less biting off their bottom lip. Yet even the experienced runners can also show signs of wanting to get rid of a nervous feeling one way or another. I say do not even bother trying to rid yourself of those shakes.

I have found that the biggest part of being nervous has to do with actually being nervous. By that I mean it is the nervous feeling itself that makes people wig out, not the actual event itself. With regard to running, I tell people that I have run over three hundred half marathons, marathons, and ultramarathons, and at the starting line of every one, I have felt butterflies. Heck, if I go more than two months without a marathon, I am a virtual wreck when I toe the line. I thoroughly enjoy speaking in front of crowds—

---

35   Boo!

which, if you do, puts you in a group of people smaller than those have run fifty-two marathons in a year. Once I am speaking, it is like magic, and there are no nerves whatsoever. Yet before I begin, I can undoubtedly feel a sense of anticipation hoping everything goes just right.

But here's the thing: I want that feeling. Why would I want to give myself a little bit of the chills before major events? Well, it's quite simple, really. Think about, as an adult, how infrequently you get to experience the emotions connected to nervousness and anxiety and trepidation that accompany something you will eventually enjoy? Getting called into the boss's office or listening to your carpenter/auto mechanic tell you how much you are going to have to pay are about the highest levels of excitement many of us feel after we reach a certain age. Those aren't even enjoyable feelings either!

There are no more proms, first kisses, graduations, or Friday night football games—for most of us, anyway. But starting a new venture is filled with so much promise and hope. Each race I run and each speech I give can go oh-so-right but also oh-my-goodness-so-bad. As such, I try to tackle as many fresh and fun things as possible to keep those feelings alive in me. Finding a way to get rid of nerves would really defeat the purpose of that tinge of liveliness. I never want to dull those emotions simply because they might be minutely uncomfortable.

> *I learned that courage was not the absence of fear, but the triumph over it. The brave man is not he who does not feel afraid, but he who conquers that fear.*
> — Nelson Mandela

So how can you still create the nervousness and thrive off it at the same time? First and foremost, you have to realize that you have that skittishness more often than not for a specific reason. For a first-time runner, for example, the nerves arise because you are taking on something that you have never done before. Using your feet, you have never propelled your body that far, ever. You have every right to be nervous! If you have run a race many times and are on the other end of the spectrum, the nerves come from the fact that you know what it takes to get to the finish line and are aware of the pain and sacrifice. For everyone in between, in all walks of life, there is the knowledge that this could be a day when you set a personal best, or it could be a day of horrific flopping. You could give a great speech, you could finally sell that widget you have wanted to sell, or you may finally figure out how to do the one dance move you have been working on so hard for so long. But until you start running, until you start building, until you start out on that new journey, you are unsure what will actually happen.

In other words, the specific reason why you are nervous is because you care. You want to succeed. You truly wish for what you are doing to go well. You have invested time and energy into creating that Soap Box Derby racer or that thesis you need to defend or any other of a number of things, and as such, you are thoroughly devoted to a successful outcome. It is easy to not get nervous when you don't care how things turn out in the end. But you want something fulfilling and good.

So embrace the nervousness. Know what it is, and refuse to let it take over your mind. Know it is there to keep you alert and on the edge. Hopefully it will remind you that you shouldn't have done stupid things like eating spicy Thai food you have never had before in your life eight hours before you get up to run. Or implementing a change in the software without a test run to make sure there aren't any bugs. Or anything else that could potentially derail your carefully laid-out plans.

My point is that the answer to the question "How do you keep from being nervous when you step to the starting line and maybe don't feel quite ready for your race, even if you are properly trained and have been down this road before?"[36] is "I don't." Or, more accurately, "I do not want to *not* be nervous."

---

36   That's a seriously long question.

Imagining what can happen is part of the wonderfulness of life.

Uncertainty pushes us to try new things and forces us to rethink ideas we've always just taken as the truth. It prompts us into innovation and adventure and reveals true character. People who are able to grab uncertainty and run with it display a sense of fortitude and strength that will shine in all aspects of their lives. Uncertainty can be an ugly thing. It can be overwhelming and overpowering and make us feel inferior. But life is still a little better when we're able to embrace uncertainty and make it a part of our daily routine.

Check out this thought experiment. Have you ever wondered if the decisions you are making in your life fall in line with what you actually want to do? The effortless way to see what you really want is to flip a coin. The result of the coin flip isn't the important issue at hand. What matters far more is that, when the coin is in the air, you immediately know which outcome you want to come true. You might be thinking you want one thing or convincing yourself of another. But instinctively, as the coin spins end-over-end, you know what outcome you hope pops up. Your gut doesn't worry about pretenses or what you *should* want. It goes right to your core and says, "I want *X*. I sure hope the coin says *X*." It's possible that how you will eventually get the outcome you want is unknown. The steps you need to undertake might be difficult or even unclear. But by simply flipping a coin, you know what you want to do. The hardest part is over. Now you must simply go about trying to figure out how to do that thing!

> *The most difficult thing is the decision to act, the rest is merely tenacity. The fears are paper tigers. You can do anything you decide to do. You can act to change and control your life; and the procedure, the process is its own reward.*
> — Amelia Earhart

The thing about uncertainty is that it sparks creativity. I can promise you, as we discussed at the beginning, the people who say they are "thinking outside the box" are not doing that at all. Pretend you don't want to use "thinking outside the hippo" from now on. What would you use? Swimming outside the pool? Cross-stitching outside the pattern? Reading Charles Dickens outside of Mrs. Popieski's assigned eighth grade advanced English class reading list?[37] My point is that if you want to find new ways to do things, remove some of the knowns. The uncertainty that arises from not being able to fall back on tried and true methods will fire neurons you haven't used in ages. This underutilized gray matter will spark new ways of thinking and acting.

One of my greatest uncertainty moments came when I went from working toward being an officer in the CIA, to accepting a job working for a running company in Utah, to ten weeks later losing that job and having no worldly idea what I was going to do to put food in my belly or advance my life. That uncertainty allowed me to go after anything and everything. It led me to my first paid speaking engagement. It laid the groundwork for my first book. It set up the career I now have, where I have combined my passions with my vocation in order to do what I can to inspire others to chase their dreams. Without that uncertainty I may have stayed in a job I wasn't happy for way too long a period of time.

So you must ask yourself, "Am I happy with where my life is heading? If not, what can I do, today, this very minute, to change that? Then, what can I do in the long term to help keep myself moving in the right direction toward accomplishing my dreams?" If you don't know, then start to get creative. Imagine no longer having the cushion of a paycheck to keep you sated. Think about how you would feel if fear was motivating you more than comfort was weighing you down.

This uncertainty will shock you back into a state of awareness. Now, suddenly, every action you make is one you think about with greater detail. Should you really be spending every lunch eating out when one lunch at a

---

37 Ain't happening, Donna. Charles Dickens sucks.

sit-down place costs as much as the groceries for an entire week of lunches if you made them at home? Is it better to sit on that email you were going to send if it is going to unnecessarily rock the boat? Why do you even care about that office gossip if it is doing nothing but slowing you down on your quest to get a better job anyway?

Now that your senses are heightened you can start paying attention to everything you do. Is what you are eating, wearing, saying, thinking, or writing going to help you get to the goal that you want? If not, why are you doing it? Can you still do that thing and press forward? Or will it slow you down? If so, stop doing it. Right now is not the time to be burdening yourself with things that do not help you. You never really know what is going to happen to you next in life, and extra baggage is not helping.

When you start to become hypervigilant, you realize that this uncertainty in your life helps breed a sense of autonomy. The absolute best way to learn how to do something is by simply doing it. You can read all the books you want and watch all the how-to YouTube videos, but until you figure out a toggle bolt anchors onto the back side of a wall, or that adding butter to the pan rather than directly to the food helps with the flavor, or any other of a myriad of things you must do to learn, you are just a collection of unproven facts.

Please don't assume I am saying that this is easy. Jumping into a pool to learn how to swim is not particularly safe or advised—but chances are you are going to learn how to keep you head afloat really quickly if you do.

> *I wanted a perfect ending. Now I've learned, the hard way, that some poems don't rhyme, and some stories don't have a clear beginning, middle, and end. Life is about not knowing, having to change, taking the moment and making the best of it, without knowing what's going to happen next. Delicious Ambiguity.*
> — Gilda Radner

CHAPTER 8
EFFORT MATTERS

As I said in the introduction, I've never been particularly impressed with myself.[38]

Please don't take this as me being modest. Modesty is extremely over-rated, in my opinion. Modesty demands the person, at best, has a moderate view of their self-worth. It is a bit of self-deception or a play on what we really think about ourselves. That is why they say one has to "act" modest. Humility is slightly better and more in line with my feelings, but to be humble means you think you have something to be humble about.

> *Don't be humble...you're not that great.*
> — Golda Meir

I am indeed proud of my accomplishments. I am happy for what I have achieved and can find solace in the fact that I give as much of myself as possible in all of my endeavors, even if I don't always succeed.[39] But whenever I have been able to accomplish anything in particular, I have a tendency to

---

38   That said, this chapter is going to be the most me-centric of the entire book, as I use myself to really drive home a point.

39   As is said, never half-ass anything. Give it your whole ass.

assume afterward that it must not be too difficult. If *I* can accomplish this, well, I surmise there must be others who can also do the same. This holds true even when no one seems to have ever done what I just got done doing. Perhaps they just haven't had the gumption to give it a shot yet, I suspect.

That said, without a doubt, I have accomplished feats most either cannot, or will not, even attempt to accomplish. For example, as you are well aware, I made a name for myself in 2006 by racing fifty-two marathons in fifty-two weekends at an effort level that, in hindsight, seems rather impossible. (I will get that that in just a minute.) Yet there are times, particularly when I am feeling out of shape after a subpar workout, that I have no idea how I was able to do those races, especially at the effort level I did them.[40] Since I finished the fifty-two, with the other events and challenges I have put myself through, I have been able to piece together parts of a puzzle to find out how it was all possible. Unfortunately, gaps still remain.

Attribute-wise I fall strongly in the above-average category for many different measurable qualities. But above-average is just about the end of it. I am not in the single digits in body fat percentage. I am not blessed with a high VO2 max. I don't clear lactic acid at a rate that makes scientists scratch their heads, like my buddy ultramarathoner Dean Karnazes. I figured there must be something else about me that makes it easier for me to excel than others. Some unknown quality that isn't measured yet must be the key to the unlocking what takes a relatively fit guy and affords him the opportunity to do things other relatively fit guys cannot do. Then I realized I was wrong.

Years after completing the fifty-two marathons as well as a plethora of other challenging physical challenges, I found out that I have Gilbert's syndrome. One of the telltale signs of GS is an extremely high bilirubin count. I had been aware of this high count for numerous years but didn't know what it meant exactly or how it could affect me. One of the first times this was made known to me was when I was interviewing for the CIA and went

---

40   I averaged 3:21 per marathon, setting a new personal best five times and going sub-3 for the first time ever in the forty-second race of the year.

through a litany of tests including extensive bloodwork. The doctor initially assumed it was because I had been drinking alcohol within the past few days, as that is one earmarks of an elevated count. The problem with that hypothesis was that I hadn't drunk alcohol since 1999, half a decade before those tests. But as having a high bilirubin count isn't a disqualifier for acceptance into the CIA, nor is it, by itself, known to be particularly dangerous, nothing further was questioned.

You see, for the most part, having Gilbert's is not necessarily a bad thing. It isn't a good thing to have, but it isn't exactly cancer. Most people don't even know they have it because they do not exert themselves in a way to be affected by it. Similarly, for a long period of time, neither had I. Then I decided to start doing extreme athletic events most do not try.

For those who don't know what Gilbert's is, basically, under periods of stress, my liver does not filter toxins as well as the normal person does. As such, while the normal person can move on from exercise in X number of minutes to perform well again, I take X plus "some more."[41] In other words, I can't do what other people can. Or, at least, I shouldn't be able to do so. In fact, some doctors would say that someone with Gilbert's would be unwise to tackle a marathon, given how much it taxes the system of even those who are physically fit and don't have Gilbert's.

One.

Marathon.

Fast-forward many years. I was getting some blood work done after a couple of hard, but not all-out, effort races for tests for something completely unrelated. These tests showed my CK levels (a chemical marker of exploded muscle cells) were that of someone who had done something much harder for much longer. The one intangible that I thought I had above others, namely being able to simply recover faster, didn't actually exist. For all intents and purposes, virtually everyone should be able to do what I do better than me.

---

41   That's the medical term. Latin is a beautiful language.

Hmmph.

So what's my point? My point is not that people should be awed by what I have done. It is the exact opposite. What prompted this thinking was the eight millionth reading of a blog, book, article, Tumblr, tweet, or Snapchat of someone putting what they had accomplished on a pedestal to be admired by all. Then they put themselves low on the ground. That way, when the pedestal was toppled, they could be revered all the more. Or they attach titles to themselves that sound lofty but are unearned. (One female marathoner I know routinely calls herself "elite" when she has a 2:56 PR. That's a solid time, but it is nowhere close to "elite." But if I point that out, *I* am the jerk.[42])

Let's not confuse my point. People should be proud of what they have done. I am the first person to stop people midsentence when they say they are "only" running a half marathon this weekend. Or they have "only" written an article and couldn't write a book. Or they have "only" been able to get their bachelor's degree. Basically, anytime "only" is uttered, I want people to think about why they use this word. I do this because instead of being self-deprecating, their achievements should be celebrated. But they should be celebrated in context. In other words, there is a bit too much back-patting going on in the world today. Plain and simple, not everyone wins all the time. And the most talented person doesn't always come out on top.

> *The successful warrior is the average man, with laser-like focus.*
> — Bruce Lee

It is OK not to be the best. Only one person can be anyway. There are degrees of achievement that don't have to be the absolute pinnacle, of which

---

42 One of the great things about running is that unlike ball sports, there are definable things that make a person elite. For women, in this example, we could use the standards that allow a woman to qualify for the Olympic trials in a marathon. The slowest time allowed for this "elite" standard is 2:47. So others are jerks.

people can still be proud. Anyone with an ounce of perspective can understand the levels of triumph without needing to make every single accomplishment a David versus Goliath battle. If everything is the most epically amazeballs thing *evah*, then by definition, nothing is. Funny enough, this could be seen as me telling people to get over themselves, but that is not the case at all. Most people do not need to get over themselves. They just need to get over the need to embellish.

What is ironic is that while I am not impressed with what I do, I am almost always moved by the achievements of others, especially if I see the effort which is given. Effort, not talent, has always been a hallmark of what I find to be most spectacular.

This effort is where you can make a difference in your life. We cannot control the DNA we have been given. We have limited to no control over the situations we inherit. But we do determine how much effort we put into making the best out of our life. We all get the same 168 hours in a week. How you spend those hours will determine where you are headed.

Take care to remember that work alone is not effort. You can work endlessly without actually putting in effort. Also, don't confuse busy with getting anything done. One of my absolute biggest pet peeves is people who claim they are busy simply because they fill the time with things that waste it. We live in a world where we hold a supercomputer in our hands virtually twenty-four seven that can text, call, email, fax, or anything else we need it to do. Yet, people spend valuable time looking at pictures of people they have never met, getting into internet fights with people they don't know, or adding cat filters to their own pictures because…honestly, the last one is completely lost on me. Somehow they are too "busy" to fill out that form you need, or pay bills on time, or actually do something productive that, in yesteryear, they could at least say they weren't in the office and therefore couldn't do it. Not today. That is why effort matters.

When people do something for me, I thank them. They often say, "Well, don't thank me yet. Nothing has happened." But the fact of the matter is that what I hope happens is often a combination of luck, other people doing something else, and happenstances out of their control. It is their effort in doing what they need to do to move it along that I appreciate more than the end result. So few people put forth this effort for themselves, let alone others, and as such, I feel it needs to be applauded.

> *What keeps so many people back is simply*
> *unwillingness to pay the price, to make the exertion,*
> *the effort to sacrifice their ease and comfort.*
> — Orison Marden

Every single thing you want to achieve has as a price attached. You must give something up (time, energy, relationships) in order to get something else. Effort matters because if you are going to be spending valuable, and sometimes irreplaceable, resources on something, why would you simply go through the motions? Your efforts must be targeted and precise in order to have the maximum impact on what you are doing.

Unfortunately, most of the time, the only way to find out the right way to assist yourself is by doing it the wrong way first. But effort is never lost when it is used in the process of learning. When you muster the energy and desire to make your life better, all steps you take will be made toward eventually reaching your goal. Of course you want the end result to be productive. Absolutely you want your product to be usable and fulfilling to you. But the only way you will get to that finish line with what you hope to have is by putting in the effort to make it happen in the first place.

CHAPTER 9
GET OFF THE SIDELINES

The secret of getting ahead is getting started.
— Mark Twain

When I left the corporate world over a decade ago, I did so in direct contrast to everything that had led me to that point previously. College begat grad school, which begat interviews with governmental agencies, which begat…fifty-two marathons in one year? Where in the heck did that come from? Wait, you are now moving to Utah and taking a huge pay cut to take a job in the running world? And now that job was rubbish, so you are going to work for yourself? Yep.

This foray into newness was not done fearlessly. For those who applaud my bravery in taking on the unknown, I am quick to tell them that half of my decisions were simply reactions to things out of my control. I am rigid, but I can adapt. Both attributes have been paramount to my steadfast decision to never work an ordinary job again. Curveballs would only begin to describe what have been thrown at me as I have done my best to move forward.

A minute part of what I have done in my career has been done with ease. Yet being here, where I am now, is worth it. If I had known it would take this long and that all I had to do was persevere, it would have been a cakewalk. But that's the point: we rarely, if ever, know when the payoff of what we work for will be. So we soldier on, hoping sometimes against hope that what we seek is just around that next corner. Here an obligatory passage about enjoying the journey on the way to the end is too easy and would be a smidgen trite. We all know we should stop and smell the roses. I hardly need to tell you this. And sometimes, honestly, those roses stink.[43]

Focusing on a goal and sinking our teeth into it, all while shrugging off the stings of arrows, is what gets many of us through each tough day. You obviously cannot ignore everything that happens to you, but being aware and reacting is different from knowing and being distracted. If you have a goal, and you think it is worthwhile, then do not let anyone or anything stand in your way.

Life, like running, rarely rewards those who sit on the sidelines.

> *Nothing in the world can take the place of Persistence. Talent will not; nothing is more common than unsuccessful men with talent. Genius will not; unrewarded genius is almost a proverb. Education will not; the world is full of educated derelicts. Persistence and Determination alone are omnipotent. The slogan "Press On" has solved and will always solve the problems of the human race.*
> — Calvin Coolidge

Earlier in the book, I mentioned my father, who was crippled in a hunting accident. Obviously this is a devastating circumstance and one that would "win" the bad story lotto in most families. My mother, however, could give my father a run for his money. Stricken with rheumatic fever as a child, she spent three of the first five years of her life bedridden. She tells me stories

---

43 Can we pause for a second to remember that in 2003, OutKast could do no more so easily that they had a hit with a song with the lyrics "Yeah, roses really smell like poo-poo-oo"?

of her younger sister dragging her around from room to room in a cardboard box as a means of transportation when she got sick of being in bed.[44] The aftermath of the rheumatic fever lead to heart problems later in life; twice, she had to have open heart surgery to replace aortic valves. On top of that, I actually added—quite accidentally—a little bit to her discomfort.[45]

When I was a senior in high school, I was active not only in athletics but also in theater. In addition I had a paper route where I had to be up at 5:00 a.m. six days a week every day from seventh grade until I graduated high school. One particular weekend I had three showings of a school play and a couple of different sporting events thrown in as well. My mom volunteered to do my paper route one morning for me on a cold, snowy northwestern Pennsylvania day, to give me an extra hour of sleep. Unfortunately, as I was trying to enjoy the extra shut-eye, it was soon interrupted by a squawking on our intercom system.[46] My mom woke me from downstairs saying she was sorry, but I had to do the paper route. She had fallen and twisted her ankle a bit and thought it might be best if I finished it. With a little grumbling, I, of course, got up to do it but was still bummed that I didn't get to sleep in. Later that day, I learned from a call from the principal's office that she had been taken to the hospital and had to get multiple screws put into her ankle for a badly broken bone. Fast-forward to a few weeks later, when I qualified for the state championship meet in swimming. Even bad weather and three feet of snow did not stop my mother, in a wheelchair, from making her way to support me at that state meet hours away.

I paint this picture to talk not about the hardships that my mother has gone through, as she will undoubtedly be quite embarrassed that I've even

---

44 This was apparently strictly verboten, but my family doesn't raise no candy-asses.

45 Not the whole being born part, surprisingly. She said that took like ninety minutes. I told her I guess I had things to do.

46 This was a little handy-dandy device we bought at Radio Shack or something that allowed us to communicate from the upstairs to the downstairs, mainly so my father didn't have to move around much. It was pretty cool. Except at five o'clock in the morning.

mentioned any of these. Like my father, my mother never allowed difficulties in life to dissuade her from doing what she needed to do. My father, even though he obviously could use one, never once applied for a handicap-parking permit because, according to him, "that's for people who actually need it."

I set the table with that story so that I can tell you another one. After being gone for a few months in grad school, I came home to visit my parents one summer for a long weekend. We had a rather modest house in a small town with a nice front yard that my parents kept extraordinarily lush with vegetation and flowers and whatnot. What hadn't been there the last time I was home was a small pond that now occupied the side yard of our house. About the size of a child's plastic swimming pool, this pond had a sprinkling fountain shooting up from the middle. Behind the pond was a two-foot-tall babbling waterfall. Trickling down through a variety of rocks and flowers, it babbled quietly into the water below.

Upon further inquiry I found out that my crippled father and mother with a bad heart and decimated ankle had built this entire pond system themselves. They were both quite handy and inventive with things around the house, so ideas such as this were not uncommon. However, when I inspected the waterfall further to fully appreciate its beauty, I saw there were some rather large rocks that made up the base of the structure. I couldn't quite understand how these two had been able to get them from wherever they had been gathered and put them in their current place.

As they explained all the work that went into the construction of this project, I was quite dumbfounded. I pressed further on the matter as to how they could have possibly done this without help. My father, a man of few words, answered my question of "Yeah, but how?" with a matter-of-fact shrug: "It took a while." Cue me shaking my head.

I started this chapter with a quote from Twain; let me end with another.

> *Twenty years from now you will be more disappointed*
> *by the things you didn't do than by the things you did.*
> — Mark Twain

My parents could have decided that while this was a great idea, there was no way they could create this pond by themselves. It easily would have taken couple of able-bodied people a few days or a week at least to complete this. Given the difficulty, they could have easily hired someone or just decided to forget about making it altogether. But they wanted a pond and a waterfall. So they got to working. I never really got around to asking them how long it actually took. The crux of the matter is that it didn't matter how long it took. They wanted it done, so they got it done. Rather than lament the length of time necessary to finish the task, they got working on it.

I like to use this simple phrase whenever someone asks me how I have gotten books published, put together a speaking career, trained for a one-hundred-mile race, or accomplished anything else that doesn't look like it could be done too quickly. How did I get it done?

Well, it took a while.

CHAPTER 10
KNOW THY ENEMY

> *Know your enemy and know yourself and you can*
> *fight a hundred battles without disaster.*
> — Sun Tzu

Mr. Sun has said some really wise things that have become part of normal everyday use.[47] In running, athletes will go to great lengths to be prepared for their races. Some wear lucky socks, and others pin their bib numbers on the same way each time. Most check the website to learn what sort of beverage will be handed out, how often they can access it, what the elevation is, and so much more. But then there are those who go into the race without even the most basic knowledge of what lies ahead. This baffles me.

The first ever speaking gig I was offered caught me completely off guard. I had no idea what to ask for in the way of compensation. I didn't want to sell myself short, but I definitely didn't want to give away my services for less than what the person speaking to me would offer for them. I knew whom the organization had hired the previous year, and therefore, without trying to be too sneaky or coy, I simply asked: "Does Previous Speaker Fella still command $X for his salary?" When they replied, "Well, that seems a bit higher

---

47   I like to pretend he had a boy named Capri, but that is neither here nor there.

than what we paid him," I at least had a framework from which to work when asking for my own paycheck. I can tell you the amount I received was far higher than what I would have asked for. Now, because I had been paid that amount, I knew I could get that much going forward, if not more. Just a scintilla of information had given me leverage in a discussion that would set me down the road I am on today.

Then again, as Einstein said, information is not knowledge. For example, a simple perusal of Yelp reviews for a restaurant website and the comments online about it can give a diner whiplash. The same thing is true for the reviews of many of the races I have run. One runner lambasting a race for one particular feature while another raves about it makes you wonder if they are talking about the same race.

Undoubtedly you have heard two people say the same thing about a movie or TV show. How can two people have such widely different viewpoints? In the end, that doesn't nearly matter as much as gathering that information in the first place. With all the details, you are that much closer to fully understanding whatever it is that you want to know about. Usually the truth of a matter lies in the middle of the two polar opposites.

When I put together the inaugural Drake Well Marathon in 2006,[48] time constraints and logistical issues kept me from having the course explore the hills, woods, and beautiful homes of my hometown of Titusville, Pennsylvania. With the initial course being 105.5 laps around my high school's track, many were heard to groan when thinking about the perceived monotony. Perhaps monotony could be a problem, but there was at least one splendid thing this course offered: no surprises. No hills popped up at mile 22, no aid stations were out of place, and no one could possibly get lost. As for mile markers, how does a marker every four hundred meters grab ya?

---

48 I put this race on as a director while running fifty-one others. I was a bit preoccupied.

My point is, when the fear of the unknown was removed and runners could concentrate solely on the act of running, so much more was a breeze. Runners qualified for Boston for the first time, set new personal bests, and figured out how powerful knowledge can be. Knowing what they did, many were able to overcome so much, which would have seemed impossible just the day before.

It is good to remember, however, that knowledge is just *potential* power. Not power in and of itself because, like with most things, if it is not acted upon, it is useless. However, accumulating information, turning it into knowledge, and then behaving accordingly are hallmarks of someone knowing their enemy and besting them.

That said, Sun made it perfectly clear that often our enemy is ourselves. If you want to know all of your enemies, you'd better learn everything you can about the one closest to you. If you don't identify your weaknesses, those who are trying to win what you have will do just that and eventually destroy you. When you have identified what needs to be changed about yourself, you have to make adjustments. If you are bad at running hills and the race has them, you'd better train on them. If your presentation will involve speaking in front of a large crowd and that terrifies you, you'd better practice. If you need to lose weight but snacking keeps you from doing so, stop buying snacks so you can't eat them.

There are a thousand examples that fit every walk of life about not only those who are trying to bring you down from the outside, but the saboteurs in your mind trying to defeat you as well. Learn everything you can about both sides of the fence. If you don't make adaptations to strengthen your front line, your foundation, your infrastructure, or your chain of command, you will lose.

There is a quote that has been attributed to so many people, I have no idea whom to accurately credit it to. So let's pretend I said this: "Stop being afraid of what could go wrong, and think of what could go right." How can you make this transition? Well, by being armed with as much knowledge as you can about whatever it is you are going to tackle, you can begin to stop worrying about the potential pratfalls and begin thinking of how to celebrate your victories. It is far easier to think about what can go right when you are not worrying about the murky waters you could have cleared.

So don't go into your next venture without the knowledge that is easily attainable about the specifics regarding the people you are working with, the lay of the land, and previous conclusions. Don't allow ignorance to stop you from achieving a much more pleasant outcome.[49]

---

49 My shortest chapter is homage to Sun Tzu's *The Art of War*, which has only six thousand words and thirty-eight pages. You don't have to say a lot to say much.

CHAPTER 11
COMPLETE; THEN COMPETE

A friend of mine once said, "Today, I signed up for a marathon six months from now. I've probably got a while before I need to get serious about my training." I thought about it for a second and told him, well, that depended. How long is a while? What does he mean by "get serious"?

This nation has become marathon crazy. This is both good and bad. One of the bad side effects of this craze is how many runners just seem to be clamoring for ways to pad their stats, especially when it comes to the simple number of marathons they have completed. Never mind the time in which those marathons were run; these runners are just looking to complete the race. They want accolades on social media and from their friends. They aren't actually looking to actually challenge themselves.

Believe me; simply completing a marathon is a big deal. There is no way I am saying it is easy to travel 26.2 miles on foot. But then once you have done so, the desire to move on, to go faster, to challenge oneself should be burning deep inside you. It is not necessarily about how fast you wish to, or can, run, but rather the desire to run faster that is the crux of the issue.

Often claims are made that those who feel certain standards for entrance into some marathons are elitist. The Boston Marathon is the gold standard for this. Outside of raising money for charity, if you want to run this coveted race, you have to run a preset time in order to do so. It is one of a very limited number of races that require such a stringent time goal. And it is wonderful that it does! We race to go as fast as we can. That's why there is a clock and not just sunshine and rainbows handed out at the end.

When it comes to racing, everyone wants to get faster. Denying this is just an outright lie. Sure, some may argue that they only race "for fun."[50] But if that is the case, and you only do so for the enjoyment, why sign up for a *race*? The free road is open 24/7/365. If all you want are kicks, there they are. But we want more from racing. When we put on a bib number, it is an unspoken contract that on that day, we will give all we have.

> *What's the point of being alive if you don't at least try to do something remarkable?*
> — John Green

I am obviously not stating that out of the gate, everyone should be a cutthroat competitor with no cares whatsoever about incremental improvement. Everything we attempt to do in life must first start at a level of basic competence. You can't pick up five balls and juggle them the first time you try. However, often after we initially start an activity, we show massive improvement. The reason fad diets ensnare so many people is that any sort of change in a person's lifestyle shows results right away. In the case of people wanting to lose a lot of weight, they have often gone from lethargy and sloth to sudden activity. Of course the pounds are going to fall off if you go from lying on the couch to chasing a group of friends for a few miles. The exact same thing will happen when you try to learn a new language, or try to take up painting, or anything else that requires skill. Yet after a while, you will plateau and maybe even backslide a bit. If your sudden forward progress, which was skyrocketing, slows a bit or even goes backward, it can be a bit

---

50   This implies that running fast isn't fun. I can guarantee you, it is an absolute blast.

of a disappointment. This is where many fall into the "good enough" trap.

We can think that going through the motions is good enough. The mere fact we are doing something should be a cause for celebration, some think. In select cases, this is true. For example, one person alone can't defeat climate change, but they can plant a tree or use less plastic. But in other instances pertinent to your own life, better effort has a large impact. Completing something at first feels wonderful, yet soon you should want to take it a step further. Not necessarily compete with your peers, although that isn't such a bad idea. Rather, more ideally, you should wish to compete with who you were the day before.

There are those who wonder why we must strive to improve. If it is good enough for today, then why shouldn't it be good enough for tomorrow? The reason we should reach for betterment is because by standing pat, we actually fall behind. Jobs change. Other people improve. Records fall. All of this happens because of progress. Doing the same thing over and over will get the same result. But in relation to those who are moving forward, your best is no longer achieving much anymore.

Note that I am not talking about trying to be perfect. In fact, I am talking about striving for the opposite of perfection: excellence. You see, perfection leaves us in a position where we forsake everything else in the quest to have no faults. Excellence is the antithesis of that mind-set. One cannot be great at everything. They can, however, endeavor to obtain a level of success and balance that allows them to excel at life.

Without a doubt, many stop themselves from pushing forward because of the fear of failure. If you have mastered a small part of something, maybe you were lucky, or maybe you are just good at that one thing. If you try for more, you might not have the same fortune. So you hedge. You are happy with what you have now. There is indeed something to be said for being content with what you have. Be aware, I am not talking about acquiring more material goods or building a bigger house just so you can store more stuff that you bought that you don't need. I am talking about taking the plunge to experience the euphoria that comes with excelling.

The human mind is especially adept at remembering the good over the bad. We gloss over terrible things that happen in our lives as a way to survive. We remember fondly past relationships, often forgetting the parts that made them "past" relationships in the first place. Our bounce-back ability as a species is pretty impressive. We adapt. We grow. We move on. Now, I won't say that we have made life in general too easy and that generations in the past were stronger. I am happy as a clam that my body doesn't need to learn how to fight polio. I may not know how to work on a car engine, but mostly that's because I was pretty sure by the time I knew how to do that, car engines would change drastically (and with the advent of electric cars, they assuredly have). I am all for having certain creature comforts that alleviate stress and unnecessary hardship. I like comfort in some parts of my life so that I can maximize the discomfort in other parts.

I ran the entire coast of Oregon, over 350 miles, in one week back in 2012. I had only run over three hundred miles in one month on two other occasions. Now I was going to do it in one week. Along the way I had a crew taking care of my hydration and food needs—a bare-bones crew but a great one nonetheless. You see, I could push myself to do something I had never come close to doing before because I was allowing myself maximum discomfort in some areas (running far) while minimizing it in other areas (allowing someone to hand me water every five miles or so). At that point in my life, I had completed 138 marathons. I knew I could cover that distance. I had run a one-hundred-miler a month before this feat to challenge myself there. But now I was competing with myself to do things I had never done before.

Virtually every day I stopped in the middle of the run to speak to a school or some other function with children about chasing their dreams. Someone asked me if anyone had ever run the entire coast before. I had, of course, looked into it when I was planning it but hadn't found anyone who had. But the fact of the matter was that it did not matter if anyone else had: *I* never had. I was competing with myself to see what was possible in my own body. I wanted to push my own personal envelope and to see where my body would fail or whether it would surprise me. I had some setbacks during that week with some really bad rain and a weird case of the vomits-a-lot. In spite of this, I was fairly certain I could cover the distance, but failure was always just around the bend. Until I crossed the Astoria–Megler Bridge into Washington State,[51] the endeavor was always in doubt. Stepping foot into the Evergreen State meant I had completed the task, competed with myself, and—at least on this day—didn't fail.

Yet the fact remains, even if everything did go wrong, I set out that week to push myself, to strain and struggle for more. Not just to collect a shiny medal and the accolades of others but to see if I could compete against my body, the elements, and anything else that came along. We unfortunately shirk away from competition sometimes as we coddle people with thoughts that everybody is a winner. Well, competition is not bad at all. In fact, competition is a wonderful thing that should be embraced.

Go give it a hug.

> *Only put off until tomorrow what you are willing to die having left undone.*
> — Pablo Picasso

Remember, we are not promised tomorrow. We are not promised this evening. Everyone who has died had something they thought they could still get done. So once you have grasped the basic tenets of whatever it is you are doing, go do more. Work harder. Stretch the limits of your soul.

It's extremely pliable, I promise you.

51　Mildly illegally, I might add. Whoops.

CHAPTER 12
THE RIGHT THING TO DO

Perhaps because a vast majority of my life has been in or around athletics, stories about sacrifice and compassion in the sports world really get to me. Without being too callous, the point of sports is to win the game. The other things about teaching leadership, growing as a person, and building friendship are all wonderful side benefits. But if you are keeping score, winning is the point. I know it doesn't sit well with people, but it's true, and I'd rather be correct than liked. Having said that, and because the point of sporting games is to win, when the other things mentioned supersede winning, they matter all the more.

Here is one such example that, a decade later, still gets me right in the heart.

In a tight basketball game, two friendly but heated rivals were playing in the second quarter of a high school game in Milwaukee, Wisconsin. Dave Rohlman's DeKalb, Illinois, team had just been awarded a technical foul. The individual who volunteered to shoot the free throws went up to the line and, according to stories written at the time, "looked at the rim. His first attempt went about two feet, bouncing a couple of times as it rolled toward the end line. The second barely left his hand."

Was he a bad player? Nope. The act was intentional. You see, Rohlman's team was awarded the shots because the opposing team from Milwaukee had inserted a player into the game who was not on the pregame roster. Was this a nefarious trick by the opposing team? Not at all. That player, Johntell Franklin, inserted into the lineup had shown up late to the game because he had, hours earlier, been at the bed of his mother, who had passed away from cancer that very same afternoon. Showing up to the game in the second quarter was a promise he had made to this team; they originally were either going to cancel or reschedule the match to show their solidarity to their team captain. He refused to let them do so and said he would arrive later if he could. As his teammates surrounded him with hugs and back pats, he surprised everyone by asking if he could join the game. His coach gladly let him into the game, which is what awarded Rohlman's team with the free throws.

After initially refusing the free throws, Rohlman was told by the referees he had to take them. A discussion went on for over seven minutes about how to handle the situation. (Insert airball shooter.)

After the first missed free throw, it became readily apparent that Darius McNeal, a senior whose hand shot up to volunteer to purposefully miss, was doing so intentionally. They stood and turned toward the DeKalb bench and started applauding the gesture of sportsmanship. Soon, so did everybody in the stands.

DeKalb ended up losing the game. But do you really care who won? As soon as you heard what happened here, you realize the score became absolutely meaningless. Rohlman had initially tried to reschedule the game himself. Then Johntell's teammates asked him if they wanted to reschedule. He said he didn't want that to happen just for him and they should play on regardless. As mentioned, Rohlman's team attempted to refuse the free throws. Finally we had a player happy to miss those free throws because it was just a sport and other things mattered more. There are so many instances of people trying to do what is right in this story that it is hard to keep count! The thing is, what is right is often so obvious. You don't need religion to tell you what to do. You don't need the fear of reprisals of man-made laws to push you in the right direction. You just need to look inward and think, *What should happen here?* When you do, you end up winning, regardless of the score.

> *The time is always right to do what is right.*
> — Martin Luther King Jr.

But let's say you need a little more you-centric reason for doing the right thing. Well, let me appeal to your self-preservation, betterment, and integrity nodes.

SAVE YOURSELF TIME

When you do the right thing, decisions become so much simpler, and they cut down on the time you spend agonizing. I have talked in this book about how the most precious commodity you have is your own time. Wasting valuable amounts on it wondering if you should choose between two or more avenues is something that can be eliminated by simply going with the one you know is right. Could it be harder? Absolutely! Often the right thing is indeed difficult to do. But now that you have saved yourself time in the decision-making process, you can spend that extra time finding the solutions to whatever it is you need to do.

ADVANCE YOURSELF

Doing the right thing will bring the right people into your life. It might not happen right away, and I can attest to that myself. Using the platform I have, I have often done what I knew was right but possibly unpopular or maybe too out there for others to join in. It has hurt me vocationally and with friends. But in my heart of hearts, when the bank account dwindled and the phone stopped ringing, I slept wonderfully knowing my actions were making the world better. Eventually those who are the right people to have in your life will show up, and you will be beyond happy you chose the course of action you did.

INTEGRITY MATTERS

If time is your most precious commodity, your integrity as a human being must come a close second. When all else fails, people will always remember that you said what you meant, meant what you said, and followed up your words with actions. Trying to build anything—be it relationships, friendships, businesses, or whatever—when you have no integrity is a one-in-a-billion shot. Sure, someone with horrific scruples will succeed, but they are the exception. You greatly increase your chance at achievements in this world by having a strong moral fiber built on making sure the correct thing gets accomplished.

LEAVING YOUR MARK

If you do the morally incorrect thing, you may possibly advance in life. Believe me, I have thought of the rebuttals to my arguments already, and I have seen terrible people do great without once thinking of anyone other than themselves. But when you do the wrong thing, someone will pay the price. The swath of destruction you leave behind you only multiplies the longer you refuse to do the right thing. And virtually no one comes out the other end unscathed. You may potentially ride high on the hog for a long time, but when it all comes back to bite you in the end, it will bite very hard. You really do tend to reap what you sow, and the crops might take a long time to run fallow, but when they do, you will starve. You will rot from not only the lack of sustainability of your actions but from the abandonment of those whom you will need to help you when you are down.

> *A candle loses nothing by lighting another candle.*
> — James Keller

So, if for no other reason than to think of yourself, think of others first. That's a shallow way to reach some people, but if appealing to one's sense of self-preservation makes them realize that their actions will have consequences, then maybe it is worth it in the end.

CHAPTER 13

STOP THE EMBELLISHMENT

I once read a story about someone overcoming some tremendous odds to run a marathon. I was pleased to hear of their success, especially for overcoming what they did. But two things about this article really irked me. Let me lay those out for you.

First, the person was dealing with a serious illness. The story was mostly about this, but a small throwaway line, whose likeness I had noticed in numerous stories with a similar theme, stuck in my craw.[52] You see, this runner had finished a marathon despite their doctor supposedly telling them they were welcome to continue training while they were ill. The doctor only posed one question to the runner when asked if the training would fit in with their surgery and subsequent medicinal therapy: "Which mile do you want to die on?" How outrageous, right?

Is it possible this was said? Sure. Probable? No. First, the claims that people pin to their doctors have always fascinated me. I am lucky enough to have a few good friends who are physicians, and as such I know their bedside manners and what they can and cannot say to people. Most of what patients claim a doctor has told them would be ethically, if not legally, wrong.

---

52   Ever had this happen? You simply cannot find a craw mechanic these days. Everything is ball bearings.

People telling stories and "journalists" writing them have used this lazy narrative for eons to encapsulate either their own perceived doubts or the accumulated doubts from naysayers they have experienced in their lives. Rather than lay out that entire history, it is easier to say, "Susie G. at Trader Joe's said I couldn't start my own hand towel business. This will show her!" Then everyone rallies behind you, because giving Susie the ole what for is what we live for. That smug Susie! I get why people do this. It moves the story forward and allows us to have a foil whom we can best. But often what was said was either completely fabricated or, at best, a gross misinterpretation of what was actually posited by someone who actually knows about which they speak.

I learned long ago that people will either be impressed with your story, or they will not. Rarely does embellishing make someone fall off the fence of opinion into your yard, where they will suddenly back you. So many tales are fascinating without the added oomph from a fib. In addition, when the fib is found out, it kills the truth.

The cousin of this type of story is the "I didn't even train and wasn't even aware this race existed until I happened across it in the middle of a training run! So I signed up and beat everyone! Let's pretend I haven't been in intense training mode for months prior to this and congratulate me for my ability to somehow be oblivious about a twenty-thousand-person race in my backyard *and* my superhuman talents!" type of story. Think I am lying? I literally, while writing this, happened over to Twitter and saw this:

"When you are a complete couch whore for a week, then you go blow out a half m'thon[53] and Garmin tells you it's a record."

Accountability is out the window. The little white lies you used to tell to five people are now things we share with the world because of social media and the need for "content." Again, perhaps this person did just set a new 13.1 personal best after doing nothing for a week. Perhaps another person never

---

53   So tired from ass kicking were they that "marathon" was too hard to type out. They only had energy for this abbreviation.

knew some something was happening, but they threw their hat into the ring and just aced it. Perhaps. But I think Marcia Brady said it best: "Sure, Jan."

The second item in the original article I mentioned that bothered me is the runner in the story says, "Racing wasn't fun. I was there to get to the finish line as fast as I could." This is something that has irked me for quite some time. The notion that running hard is not fun always seems to come from a certain segment of the crowd. A segment that permeates all walks of life, athletic or not. One who wants praise for doing next to nothing. They won't stop until they get it either, regardless of what amount of truth needs to be bent.

Let's face it. We live in a world where many runners are not running the races they run anywhere close to their potential. People are not working to their strengths in any facet of life. As I mentioned in an earlier chapter, completing is celebrated more than competing. Now I was about to say, "That's fine." But I erased it and started over. It is *not* fine. As I said before, there are instances when just getting to the finish line is admirable. But continuing to just get to the finish line without remotely pushing your limits should rarely be applauded. That said, in this instance, my beef is more with the idea that running fast is mutually exclusive from having fun.

You can have fun at almost any pace you want. Watch the video of US Olympic marathoner Deena Kastor winning the bronze medal in the Athens Olympics, and tell me if she is not the most overjoyed person ever. It had been twenty years since an American woman had won any medal in the marathon at the Olympics. Kastor ran an incredibly well-paced race in temperatures that soared above 95 degrees. She undoubtedly wanted to get to the finish as fast as she could, it being the Olympics and all. But when you watch the video, you see she is so overcome with happiness that she is in tears even while she is still running the race!

Personally, when I set my marathon personal best, I was so overjoyed, I was waving to the crowd in the homestretch. I was fortunate enough to know the announcer, who had been aware I would be shooting for a new best that day as well. As I neared the finish, he announced to the crowd over the loudspeakers what I was about to accomplish. The crowd began to cheer loudly. I had finally, after three 2:51:*xx*, run a sub–2:50 marathon. I was ecstatic. The crowd saw my joy and echoed it.

My point here is not to denigrate the subject of the article. In fact, I think it is wonderful what she did, and when you read she set a new PR in what was probably her last marathon ever (because of her terminal illness), it is even more awe inspiring. However, following the points I have delineated above, I know that the tale could be so much better.

I know it sounds like I am nitpicking. That is not my intention. But when you are watching a show or movie and the people in it do something glaringly wrong in a field you are a specialist in, it almost ruins the entire thing for you. That is how it is for me and reading other writers' articles. As an eternal sap, I am already ready and able have my heartstrings pulled. But I also know that the music from those strings is so much sweeter when the song being played is done so with defter hands.

> *Embellishment is an irresistible and consuming impulse, going back to the beginnings of human history. Probably the strongest motivating force is the simplest: the inability of almost everyone to ever leave well enough alone.*
> — Ada Louise Huxtable

Allow me another example. In another article I read how the author was touting a literal cross-country running route in Spain. In the piece, the author makes a grand gesture of how they suddenly quit their job, went home that night, and bought a plane ticket so they could leave the next day for Spain. Upon arriving in Spain, they set off with nary a plan to run the length of the country. I am exaggerating absolutely none of those details.

Having flown approximately five hundred thousand miles in the past half of a decade, I know a thing or two about air travel. I know price points and the availability of plane tickets because I am always looking for a good deal. Upon hearing this supposed spur-of-the-moment trip, I was already heading into this article a teensy bit more than skeptical about what I was going to read next. I tried not to be wary but it is like when your friend starts telling a BS story about something that happened and you were there. Total side-eye.

The author then goes on to speak about how they had little more than a passport, a spare pair of running clothes, and a backpack on their person. The skeleton of an idea was to run this fifty-mile route in a few weeks and then head back home. Or something. It really doesn't matter what the actual stated purpose was supposed to be. Why? Because by this point, the story feels like one of a thousand I have read where the author supposedly spontaneously does (fill in the blank), and we as the readers are expected to buy the story whole hog.

I despise this type of writing.

With the proliferation of blogs and social media and the like, everyone can try to tell a story. This is wonderful in so many ways. For example, hidden talent is no longer hidden because it can't find an agent or an outlet. However, a sheer amount of writing out there is chaff. Just because one can hit keystrokes doesn't mean they are a good writer.[54] As such, given the breadth of writings, this can lead to much exaggeration in order to make one person's story more grandiose than the others.

One of the things I have prided myself on when it comes to writing race recaps or tales of my adventures is to undersell what I have done. I go out of my way to keep any exuberances to a minimum. However, if anything unnatural occurs, I do my best to back it up with tangible evidence. If I say that I got cut off at the finish line by a rude competitor rolling over the finish line with three other buddies arm in arm, it is rather vindicating when the

---

54   As an FYI, I constantly feel like a fraud when I write, wondering why anyone could possibly want to read my musings. I expect at any moment to never sell another book and have zero people click any link to any post I write.

pictures arrive and shows that is exactly what happened.[55]

With the article I was reading, it was clear the author's main point was to wax poetic about this particular trail. But barely buried in the subtext was how wonderfully carefree this author was supposed to be. Sticking it to the man, throwing caution to the wind, and taking on Spain, come what may. Look at me! I am bucking convention! My bank account is obviously limitless, and my talent and skills so high I needn't prepare physically or gather proper gear, route planning, or provisions! Be inspired by my awesomeness!

Of course, the author didn't come close to finishing the entire run. Some injury flared up, and they called it quits after about eight days of running, halfway across the trail. But that doesn't matter in today's hyped world. Talk about what you are going to do, and you will get press. Hype up your adventure with a slick website or corporate funding, and many will forget that you never actually accomplished what you were getting all the attention for in the first place. Better yet, be vague about what you are trying to do so no one can ever say you failed. Couple your efforts with fund-raising, and you become bulletproof. Only the mean-spirited would ever point out you actually accomplished next to nothing and we all just paid for your vacation to Hawaii to run a marathon. By the way, what were you raising awareness for again?

The biggest problem I have with this type of storytelling is, even if it does inspire, it often will do so in a foolhardy way. The thought process being that if the average Joe can just pick up and conquer the world, then others feel they can too. In the abstract, this is a wonderful idea. In reality, it can lead to disaster or at least massive failure. More often than not, however, tales of adventure have simply paved the way for a defeatist attitude. Many stop before they even start. Having seen this firsthand, let me explain.

When I speak about running fifty-two marathons in fifty-two weekends, eventually not only just completing the marathons but running them faster than I had ever run a marathon before, I see many who are inspired to take

---

55   I literally have the photographic evidence of this chicanery.

on challenges. Unfortunately, I also see some who grasp the magnitude of the endeavor, and it frightens them. They immediately shirk any notion of chasing their dreams. "I could never run fifty-two marathons!" They are missing the point of seeing someone do something challenging.

I therefore specifically point out my undertaking was to challenge myself. It was not to compare myself against others or to try to break a world record. It was to push myself past my previous limitations. I tell them not to think about running marathons but rather to think about something, anything, they currently think they can't do. Start a business. Run a race. Become a parent. Hopefully what I have done will put them in the right frame of mind to tilt against their own windmill.

> *When you're just singing a beautiful melody with a story that's true to the heart, you don't need a lot of embellishment.*
> — Emmylou Harris

The point is to inspire, lift up, and motivate. I make a sincere effort to show how much planning, hard work, and preparation went into not only the running of the marathons but the living of my life in between the races. That is why I say I have such distaste for the type of writing or storytelling that glosses over those important details. The task that gets the headlines is usually the easiest part of the entire excursion. Lost is all the behind-the-scenes stuff many never think about.

In other words, live so no embellishment is needed. If your tale is worth telling, it will resonate so much better if it isn't filled with hot air.

CHAPTER 14

CLOSURE

We are often searching for closure. We hope for that final email that wraps everything up in a neat little bow. We crave a conversation that answers our questions as to why something went from wonderful to nasty. The problem with this particular desire is that, unfortunately, closure doesn't really exist. Instead, what we are actually hoping to procure is a time machine. We want to go back to a time before whatever went askew and stop it from ever occurring. A DeLorean but for the heart. Or, on the other hand, if we can't fix things at the Enchantment under the Sea Dance, we at least want the other person to disappear in the picture of happiness along with us.[56] But this is mostly impossible.

However, humans function mostly because we are always searching to beat the impossible.[57] Today's impossible is tomorrow's hard and next week's accomplished. We can't fault people for wanting to go after what they think will make them feel better. The fact of the matter is that we fight hard for what we truly want, ferociously so, until such time as we realize that no amount of fighting, pleading, persuading, or working will get us that thing.

---

56   That was way too many *Back to the Future* references. Alas, I am sure I have more in me.
57   Sounds like a good title for a book.

Then, finally, we move on. We can't time travel. But we can wait.[58]

If you are a talker, you hope closure will allow you to talk yourself through it all. If you are a listener, you hope closure will mean you don't have to have a heavy conversation anymore. For some of us, we simply want a fast-forward button to get us to where the healing begins.

Time will eventually dull the intense, pleasurable memories you have of the situation you are yearning for and allow you to move on. That sounds harsh, but it doesn't mean you forget those who meant something to your life. On the flip side, time also smooths out the bad memories. It relieves us of the hurt and anguish. It removes the sting of losing a loved one. It allows us to heal. Again, we don't forget but instead become stronger and more immune to the pangs of memory, which we hope to conceal.

Human connection is tenuous. I remember one of the funniest *The Onion* articles I ever read: "18-Year-Old Miraculously Finds Soulmate in Hometown." It was then topped by "Soulmate Dropped for New, Better Soulmate." Look, I am not saying that whomever you love deeply is not in fact someone that you love deeply. But unless you believe in fate (which I unequivocally do not) you have to realize that we can create strong personal connections with people who just happen to be in our general vicinity. It doesn't make them any less real or strong. But they are, at least mildly, connections of convenience. And just as tight as they were at one point, they can eventually fade.

Often there is no real reason. The connection just frays. People grow apart, and no one is to blame. The hope that one more conversation will provide answers to your questions is fraught with peril. Someone is probably going to guilt someone else, or trying to make another run at the relationship, or even worse, try to stay "just friends." The latter almost never works. People mostly part ways with one person still feeling attachment. Just being friends with someone you love intensely and watching them go on to do the

---

58   This is essentially time travel, but we don't control the direction, and it moves exactly the same speed as everyone else.

same with someone else is just a torture that no one needs.

But you can use the *idea* of closure to better yourself. If there is something you may have done wrong, now would be the perfect opportunity to apologize for any offending behavior. Make the other person know that the blame was on you. Doing this will help you become a better person not only for the present moment but also for your interactions down the road with others. The changes you make will hopefully keep you from making the same mistakes again.

This growth is how you can actually get something that is as close to a healthy closure as possible. It won't be where you somehow fix things that went wrong but rather give you the guidance so that moving forward, you will have learned from your life experiences and act differently. In the article from *The Onion* about the better soul mate, the authors really do boil down the essence of the human experience in their own snarky way. It alludes to how we can be perfectly content one day and then ready to move on the next when something else that seems to fit us much better appears.

People long for explanations. We search for meaning to our existence and the choices we make. When we find no causes that influenced our decision, we say we went with our gut or used our intuition. Sometimes this is based on past experiences, but often it is just a feeling. If we accept that there is often no rhyme or reason to our choices, and we take lessons and try to shape a better decision next time, then that is the truest of closures.

Closure is when raw memory blurs to become the folklore of life.
— Stewart Stafford

In the end, when we can't get closure from someone else, it is almost always because they themselves can't find it. So instead, give it to yourself. Accept that there are often no answers, that many things don't make sense, and that logic and reason rarely rule the day. Allow mystery to overtake you; let the unknown soak into your veins, and then dust yourself off. Each day presents you with a new chance to write your own story, and there is no sense trying to write over a page that is cluttered with typos, scribbles, and errors.

Grab some fresh paper, and write away!

CHAPTER 15
TOUCH WITH PURPOSE

Humans need to be touched. In order for us to properly grow as people and flourish into adulthood, the ability to feel the touch of other people is essential to our survival. Without it, we simply are not the same. When people are denied touch for too long, we develop what is called skin hunger—a deep longing and aching desire for physical contact with another person. Of all of the senses, touch is considered the first we acquire. In addition, our skin is our largest sensory organ. To be deprived of that which the body and mind most need changes us in ways that are still being discovered.

Scientists began investigating skin hunger shortly after World War II. In controversial experiments run by American psychologist Harry Harlow, infant rhesus macaques were separated from their birth mothers and given the option of two inanimate surrogate "mothers"—one made out of wire and wood and another covered in cloth. The baby monkeys overwhelmingly favored the embrace of the cloth surrogate, even when the wire mother was the only surrogate that held a bottle of milk. From this, Harlow deduced infant macaques needed more than nourishment from their mothers to stay alive. He termed it "contact comfort." As a result of Harlow's research, we now know that human beings need touch, particularly in childhood, almost as powerfully as they need basic necessities like food and water.

Think about that. Of course we need sustenance. But we also require to be touched by others in order to be fulfilled beings.

You may have seen videos of people on the internet or even personally on the street carrying signs that read Free Hugs. While there are a variety of places where this idea of giving out free embraces to strangers began, it is likely to have started with the Free Hugs Campaign. This social movement involving individuals started simply in Australia in 2004. An Australian man who goes by the pseudonym Juan Mann[59] began giving out hugs in the Pitt Street Mall in central Sydney. Soon thereafter, the hugs exploded across all continents. Where and why did this begin?

In the months prior to Mann taking on this social experiment of sorts, he had been feeling depressed and lonely as a result of numerous personal difficulties. However, a random hug from a stranger made an enormous difference in his well-being. Mann stated he started giving out free hugs mostly because, at the time, he had nobody around him to share any level of intimacy. "No one hugged me or socialized with me," Mann said. "Then out of nowhere, this young woman came up to me at a party and hugged me. For the first time in months, I felt alive. It got me thinking about all the other lonely people out there in the world who might need or want a hug." Surprisingly, even though hugs are usually meant for those we know and care about, the Free Hugs Campaign has centered around mostly reaching out to strangers. Moreover, it carries no sexual connotation, which is important for a few reasons.

Many people when feeling lonely try to sate their desire for touch through sex, but studies have shown that skin hunger isn't actually a sexual need. Rather, instead of just pleasures of the flesh, this type of hunger is a complex mixture of meaningful physical contact with another person that goes far beyond intercourse. Human touch is so profound that isolating yourself from it can lead to myriad problems. Virtually none of those problems are solved by the physical act of having sex. Instead, the relief comes

---

59   OK, this is one of the first videos I ever saw distributed widely on the net, even before YouTube, and writing this right here right now is the first time I realized his name was "One Man." I could have kept this to myself and hidden my shame, but you, dear reader, deserve better than that. Mock away.

from the stimuli associated with caring and nurturing that come from feeling the warmth of someone's skin on your own.

As the world becomes more automated, the problem of skin hunger continues to grow. Connecting on Facebook isn't the same as meeting someone for lunch and giving them a pat on the back. In fact, three out of every four people in America agree that they suffer from skin hunger, which is more than any other time in history.[60] We are so much more connected as a global society, but at the same time, we're the most disconnected we have ever been.

We all desire different levels of affection from those around us. Some people are very touchy-feely, while for others one handshake is enough for a month. The problem is that, unless you are getting your needs for skin hunger met, you might be living a life that has you feeling unwanted or abandoned.

Having said all of that, we shouldn't think that a hug alone or a handshake will fix our problems. Because touch is so intertwined with being a human, you should put forth a concerted effort to have the touch you lend to another have a legitimate purpose. Give that touch some weight, and make it matter.

If you are giving a handshake to someone, make sure that you do it so they know you mean it. I am not talking about crushing their hand in some ridiculous show of machismo and strength. Rather, make that handshake something of import. Let them feel the energy flowing through you. Connect with another person in a way that is both intimate but also completely appropriate.

If you are kissing a loved one, this is obviously something that goes above just a mere touch. But often, especially as time goes by in a relationship, a kiss can just become a peck. With virtually no feeling, these kisses become almost a perfunctory task to make sure the missus doesn't yell at

---

60 I could have completely made that statistic up, but look around, and if you disagree that it is likely the actual percentage is lower, you get your money back on this book. (Confers with lawyers.) No. No, you cannot actually get your money back. My bad.

you for not giving her a smooch on the way out the door. Never kiss like that again.

Of course, not every kiss needs to be a full make-out session, and for the love of Mufasa, don't do that in public. But kiss with feeling. Even in a two-second kiss, you can convey to your partner that you want them, you need them, you love them, and that you have found a lip groove with them that you will never share with anyone else.[61]

Whether you are placing a hand on the shoulder of a coworker who has lost a family member, giving a smackaroo on the cheek to your kid as you pick them up from kindergarten, high-fiving a teammate for a well-placed shot, or squeezing the hand of your loved one as you walk through a crowded area to let them know that you are with them, make sure your touches mean something. Take pride in this gift you can give to others. Allow the most intimate of things—having your skin and your touch mingling with the essence of another being—to be something of the greatest importance.

> *Touch seems to be as essential as sunlight.*
> — Diane Ackerman

Dr. Terry Kupers, a psychologist and author who has spent decades testifying as an expert witness on behalf of those in solitary confinement, has seen the effects of skin hunger firsthand. "Physical contact is a requirement of being human," says Kupers. "There's something healing about it. [Touch] is not just correlated with being human—it is being human."

Kupers is allowed to shake prisoners' hands when examining them in the state of Mississippi, where he often testifies. "When I touch a prisoner at the Mississippi isolation unit, they tell me, 'You're the first person I've touched except for officers putting handcuffs on me. Aside from that, nobody has

---

61   Not unlike Homer Simpson's butt groove on his couch. Mmmm, butt groove.

touched me in all the years I've been in solitary confinement."'

Besides prisoners in solitary confinement, there is another demographic that illustrates the debilitating effects of skin hunger: the elderly. Being extremely lonely can amount to a chronic medical condition, and it's one that is more likely to surface later life as friends and family members die off. One study found that isolated people aged fifty and over were twice as likely to die as their nonlonely peers. The case has been made that the elderly need prolonged physical contact more than younger generations: Given that normally, as you age, you become more infirm, physical contact becomes increasingly important for good health.

That means you have in your possession a gift you can constantly give without ever losing it. You can, with your one small hand, change the entire course of a day for someone else. Doing so requires you only think about how much power you have and what you can do to help others who might not even know they need it.

To borrow from the 1980s-era AT&T slogan, reach out and touch someone.

CHAPTER 16
SET YOUR OWN AGENDA

The final marathon of my fifty-two in a year ended up on New Year's Eve. In fact, that last race began at 3:00 p.m. on New Year's Eve, which is a rather unusual time to start a race. I, however, loved that starting time. I am not a morning person whatsoever, and being able to sleep in, eat a nice lunch, let it digest, and *then* run a marathon was a rare treat. I finished a little over three hours later, taking third place overall in what was a relatively understated finale for this ambitious endeavor. I wasn't really expecting fireworks or anything, although a few hours later, Springfield, Missouri, provided them anyway. I am fairly certain they weren't for me.

After calling my folks back home to tell them my yearlong feat had been completed, I hustled off to my hotel because I had a phone call with BBC Radio in London. I don't remember exactly how they had heard about my story. However, with it being after midnight in England, they wanted to call and wish me a Happy New Year from that side of the pond and inquire about my just-finished achievement. I barely had enough time to gather myself from the race and make it back to my hotel to field the call. Once there, I proceeded to have a wonderfully pleasant chat with some British chap who asked me many of the questions I had fielded numerous times all year long. This time I got to answer them with the entire undertaking accomplished, which was a nice thing to do. However, as we were wrapping up the conversation, he hit me with one that made me laugh out loud:

"So, Dane, what's next?"

To say that I was more than a little flummoxed would be an understatement. Here I was still caked in sweat from accomplishing something that I didn't think was possible. I hadn't even taken a shower, let alone gotten food in my belly, and was already being asked what I thought I was going to do *next*. I think I said something super witty and ready for sound bites like "Take a shower." Yet in my mind, I came upon a resolution right then and there to never let anyone else set my agenda again. That has been one of the biggest secrets of my happiness and success ever since.

So how do you go about following that advice and setting your own agenda?

FIRST AND FOREMOST, LEARN TO SAY NO

> *The difference between successful people and very successful people is that very successful people say no to almost everything.*
> — Warren Buffett

Most people want to help others. We don't want to be seen as unhelpful or unmotivated. Unfortunately, there still remain only twenty-four hours in each day. A few years ago, before social media, the number of people we came into contact each day was limited. But now it is vast. People will reach out to you for your time, your thoughts, and your money. But all of those things are sorely limited. By saying "no" you are actually being respectful. You are putting a limit on how much you can do, which tells people with whom you actually work that you value the connection with them. Similarly, you are not creating a false impression of what you can do for others. They can't be let down in the end because you were unable to fulfill the duties you promised; you have more or less told them to find someone who can actually do it the way they want it done.

But the key is to actually say "no." Don't leave a query unanswered. Don't hem and haw over your answer. Be kind but firm. If someone is unable to handle that, well, they need to grow up.

START SAYING YES TO YOU

The word "selfish" has a negative connotation that it shouldn't carry. Being concerned with yourself should be your number one priority. If you are not fully taking care of yourself, then you can hardly be of assistance to others. Obviously, only taking care of your needs to the exclusion of others is not a good idea either. But a car can't take people to all the places they need to go if the tires are flat and there is no gas in the tank. Think about what you need in order to bring the best out of yourself, and do that. By doing so you open the door to being able to put your best foot forward to help those you wish to assist.

We often hear of the family member who sacrifices their health by working their fingers to the bone so their children can have a better future. The sentiment here is undoubtedly a good one. But the execution is incorrect. Anyone would agree that a few more minutes with a loved one will exceed most things they could give through another hour at the office. Taking care of yourself is the unsurpassed way to ensure you can come to the aid of those who matter to you.

QUIT MAKING COMPARISONS

So much of what happens to and around us today is weaved into social media. We see the Instagram pictures of people on their vacations or the marathon medals of our high school friends or the graduations of children with high honors and immediately compare the best of other people to the worst of ourselves. How can that twenty-four-year-old already have his own business? Why are the Hendersons going to Prague when I can't afford to go to a concert? I want to make that soufflé!

Just stop. You aren't other people. Their goals are not yours. Their talents are not yours. Their bank account (or how much they went into debt for that new car) is not yours. The only thing you need to be concerned about is whether you are a better you today than you were yesterday. Some days you will be, and some days you won't. Find out why you didn't improve today, and apply it to tomorrow.

Without a doubt there are those who are envious of things in your life as well.[62] The whole grass-is-greener ideology has never been truer. You have to appreciate what you possess even if it is not yet what you want. When you look at what others have or do or own, you don't know any of the backstory. There is so much going on beneath the surface that worrying about the tip of the iceberg alone does you no good.

Embrace your individuality. Relish in what makes you uniquely you. If you flip the focus of what you are craving into something you have, now you are making the right comparison. You can see what it took to get what seems like a minor thing to others. You know the hours that went into acquiring that talent or skill. Realize that many will never understand how much time it took to achieve what you have. Then smile inwardly, knowing you have a little secret. Now stop wasting time worrying about others!

---

62   Not jealous. *Jealous* is so often misused today, I almost wrote it myself. "Jealousy" is the emotion related to fear that something you have will be taken away by someone else. "Pedantic" is someone lecturing you about grammar in a footnote.

FOCUS ON TODAY

If you view each day as the only day you are given, which it is (in fact, this minute right now is the only one you have), you will be far less concerned with what is going to happen six months from now. I am not saying you shouldn't plan ahead. If you live each day like it is your last, pretty soon it will be. Rather, when you are in the moment, it is easier to realize how important your plans are to you because they are what you are focusing on right now. It is perfectly fine if you haven't caught up on all the latest episodes of *The Walking Thrones of Deadwood* yet. You might not be where you want to be in your weight loss plan, but you will be on the way if you put *this* cookie down.[63]

Let me clarify I am in no way saying you need to be an island, isolated from everyone else with only your own survival as the key component of your life. Absolutely, your plans must have some sort of long-range component to them. And looking around you once in a while to see what others are doing will sometimes help steady your ship. But you have to realize that there truly is only one person who can do the things you need to do for yourself, and it is the one inside your own body.[64] You have to control your actions, grab hold of the reins of your own life, and make sure you hold tight.

You deserve to control your life. Don't let anyone else create your calendar for you.

---

63 How awesome is it going to be when someone is eating a cookie when they read this?

64 Fun fact: We are in a virtual tie in our own bodies with the number of microbes that are not us, meaning that we are almost more not us than us. Enjoy your sleep tonight!

CHAPTER 17

I DON'T KNOW

> *Maturity, one discovers, has everything to do*
> *with the acceptance of "not knowing."*
> — Mark Z. Danielewski

Studies have been conducted about why it becomes harder to learn a new language as we grow older. In fact, it is said the best time to learn any language happens before the age of ten, long before many become even remotely proficient with it. While the hippo[65] is out on why this is exactly the case, some believe the lack of adaptability of the brain with age has nothing to do with a declining feature or lack of ability to learn but rather more with hubris. In order to learn something, we have to admit, at least subconsciously, that we do not know that thing. When we become older, we have less of a tendency to be able to do so, making it harder to learn.

Ever have a friend who always seems to have the answers even when they don't? You ask if they have heard about something that just happened in the news, and instead of saying they hadn't, they have to seem up-to-date and reply, "Yeah, that thing in Syria, right?" Of course, it happened in Ireland, and they are all, "Wait, yeah, that's what I meant." It is embarrassing for

---

65   You seriously didn't forget about the hippo, did you?

most people to not know what is happening or to admit they are unaware of whatever is being talked about.

Rid yourself of that fear. Again, as mentioned earlier, think like a child. How does admitting you are ignorant, in the true sense of the word, help you get ahead? Here's how.

GAIN KNOWLEDGE

Instead of pretending you know how to do something and then later realizing you don't, if you admit up front what you aren't aware of—blam! You get the information right there. This cannot only be something that saves you a lot of time but also a great deal of money. If you don't know how to fix the garbage disposal, sure, maybe with an online tutorial you can look to see if a spoon is caught in the grinders, but other than that, call a freaking plumber.[66]

Lost in a strange town and don't know where you are going? Ask for directions. Even if you somehow do have an innate sense of direction, no one is that impressed that you somehow fluked your way through the bad part of town without a GPS, Magellan. All anyone cares about is arriving safely at or around the time that they were supposed to be there.

Even if you are fairly certain about something, no one is an expert on anything. Plus, things change. One of the worst things about the bar exam in law school is how it tests your ability to memorize as much as possible. But in real life practice, lawyers would never rely on whether something they learned years ago was still true. They would make sure the law hasn't been updated by essentially asking questions of their resource materials. Refreshing your brain at the fountain of knowledge is never a bad thing.

---

66   And possibly save your fingers in the process.

FORM STRONGER BONDS

Even if you do happen to know a great deal about things and are doing your best to be helpful, people can often be turned off by the fact that you seem like a know-it-all. While you shouldn't fake your knowledge and play dumb, chances are high someone else knows roughly the same amount as you do about whatever is being discussed. Let that person speak. Befriend them. Find out how they learned what they did, and increase your knowledge. If it ends up that they had the same conclusion as you did, then fantastic! Now two people agree, and someone else got a share of the credit for once.

You become more relatable if you aren't always infallible, and that makes people want to be around you more. They probably will still come to you for advice and trust you as their walking Google search, but now they also see you as enjoyable. Moreover, if you have a project you want people to help with, nothing will get them more invested in helping you out than feeling like they are actually contributing.

In the end, people know who has expertise and will come to those who know the most anyway.

TAKE A BREATHER

Back to that friend who pretends to know everything. Man, that has to be exhausting. To keep up this charade, you have to always be ready with an excuse if you don't know what is going on. That is no way to live. Eventually what is going to happen is people won't believe these people, even if they do know what is being talked about. So if someone asks you about something and you don't know, just admit you don't know. They will probably bring you up to speed in about two sentences, and then you can move on and join in the conversation. You can't know everything.

But yeah, if you haven't ever seen *The Shawshank Redemption* and they reference it, lie about it, you cretin.[67]

IT'S GOOD FOR YOU

Intellectual humility—recognizing the limits of your knowledge and valuing the insight of someone else—is exceedingly helpful to the learning process. Nobel Prize-winning astrophysicist Subrahmanyan Chandrasekhar noted, believing that you "must be right"—in other words, lacking intellectual humility—can actually stymie discovery, learning, and progress. Studies have borne this to be true. It is almost the opposite of the Dunning–Kruger effect, which is the bias where people mistakenly assess their cognitive ability as greater than it is. In other words, the less information people have about something, the more often they have a greater faith in their ability to know what is going on. With this effect we get congresspeople bringing a snowball into Congress in February trying to disprove what every climate scientist in the world says about climate change. Because apparently "Well, I'm no scientist…" is now considered to be a perfect rebuttal to something about science.[68]

Mastering all of the above tools will show you how you can quickly and easily turn "I don't know" into knowledge. You can create new pathways to friendship. You can revitalize your own thoughts and ideas by admitting you can't possibly retain everything all at once. Ignorance—that lack of knowledge so many people see as a weakness, and for which we all have been mocked for at one point in our lives—is actually a sign of strength and intelligence.

Be a supersmart, strong person instead. It doesn't come with a cape, but that's OK![69]

---

67 Seriously, how have you not seen that?
68 Don't be Congressman Snowball.
69 I mean, it could come with a cape. That's on you.

CHAPTER 18
LOSE WEIGHT

N
o, this is not a chapter about how I am going to help you lose those stubborn ten pounds in just two weeks in time for your neighbor's daughter's quinceañera! Although, if we are being honest, the vast majority of us could stand to tone up by a touch, present company included. In fact, I have often struggled with my own weight, even as an endurance athlete. While I was quite thin in high school, mostly due to teenage metabolism and playing three sports a year,[70] that came to an end soon after graduation. Running has helped me a great deal with battling the weight, but if I don't make a concerted effort with diet and exercise, as I am past forty years of age now, it all balloons up.

That said, I am actually speaking more about the things that weigh us down mentally and physically, which have nothing to do with calories and fudge and soda pop. Marie Kondo has made a huge splash with her idea of tidying up. To me (and everyone I talked to who couldn't figure out why this was such a revelation), it seemed like such an obvious solution. Get rid of things in your life that don't add value. Then again, if people followed logic and reason all the time, the world would be a more wonderful place, and you wouldn't be reading this book. But humans are made of all kinds of weird gut

---

70 With a morning paper route, theater practice after school, and shivering just to stay warm eight months out of the year in my chilly northwestern Pennsylvania town.

feelings and emotions and nonsensical actions. I guess it keeps life interesting. However, it can weigh you down.

Start this mental weight loss program with things that are dead weight. Get rid of the people who drag you down. Now, here I am not talking about toxic people. We all know who these people are, and by and large, most of us stay away from them. But, hey, you know what—this is an all-purpose book to help you with everything, so let's address those people too!

> *No one can make you feel inferior without your consent.*
> — Eleanor Roosevelt

Toxic people try to control you. Usually these people have no control over their own day-to-day stuff, so instead they try to assert regulations over yours. By forcing check-ins, requiring phone calls, or making your schedule fit theirs, they work to make sure the hold that have on you is strong. Some do this act of restraint through overt methods. Others, the really skilled ones, do it through subtle manipulation.

Toxic people take. What do they take? Everything. Your time, your energy, your money, your thoughts, your patience, the end of a mallet to the back of their skull if they push you too far.[71] They also never give anything back but things you don't want. They give you grief, anxiety, headaches, ulcers, a large cleaning bill to get the blood out of the carpet from the mallet.[72] In spite of this, there are many well-meaning people who wish to fix these toxic atrocities, and therefore, they put up with this behavior. But you need to treat toxic people like bad fruit. You absolutely cannot fix bad fruit. You can fix a remote control that breaks. You can put duct tape on a table leg that's splintered. But once fruit goes bad, the only thing you can possibly do

---

71   Kidding. Don't hit people with hammers, kids.
72   Seriously, no hammers. This isn't *Looney Tunes.*

is bake it into bread.[73] So when someone is toxic, the best way to think about them is as if they are a brown and mushy banana. Adios, nanner.

Toxic people are easy to identify because they accept no responsibility and are always right. Even when they are clearly wrong, they will just invent a reason why they aren't. Inherent in this character trait is a lack of honesty. Whether it is habitual lying or just lying for convenience, many see playing you to be akin to playing a game. Refuse to be player number two in Toxic Solitaire.

The one thing that allows good people to let toxic people back into their life, bad nanner and all, is when they play the martyr. The "woe is me" card gets whipped out faster than the Draw Four card in Uno when you are playing with your older brother. Do not allow them to guilt you or toy with your emotions by declaring that they are the victim and no one understands them. Tell them you do understand them, and you understand they need to get out of your life.

So, for the love of sanity and hippos, remove these people first and foremost from your interactions, large and small. Yes, they might be your sister or your cousin, but unless you absolutely have to be there for them (and for the most part, you don't), don't let the fact that they are family alone keep you trapped in an unhealthy relationship.[74]

Now that we have that out of the way, let's talk about the other things that don't seem as bad, but like an extra Twinkie now and then, really start to add weight.

---

73   Do not bake toxic people into bread.
74   "Blood is thicker than water" is the stupidest phrase. You can't choose your family members. Why should you be stuck with them just because you share some of the same DNA?

> *Toxic people attach themselves like cinder blocks tied to your ankles, and then invite you for a swim in their poisoned waters.*
> — John Mark Green

First we move on to those who are annoying, difficult, demanding, or otherwise unpleasant. Again, ask yourself, "Do I *need* to have this person in my life?" If the answer is no, then remove them. Our time on earth is so short.[75] Why spend any of it with people who don't put a check in the "pros" column in your life?

You often cut this weight from your life by simply communicating your boundaries. Many people get so offended when you simply state your wants and desires that they will remove themselves. Somehow something like "Hey, just to be up front, I'd prefer to not spend time gossiping about others" is seen as such an affront that they won't bother with you anymore. Win-win!

Often many of us try to not be rude by sacrificing our own happiness so we don't bother someone else. Well, knock that off right now. Instead of confronting the person, we think they will go away if we ignore them or pretend they don't bother us. This has happened exactly one time in human history.[76] So be bold and take the initiative. If this isn't a circumstance where simply ignoring them on the subway or at a bar won't remedy the situation, then take action. The momentary uneasiness you feel at the time will be multiplied back a thousandfold in the unhappiness you don't have to spend in that person's presence any longer.

The biggest weight that you can cut out of your life comes with relationships with loved ones that have come to an end. Look, if I knew how to solve heartache and why we go back to the ones who hurt us, I would have bottled

---

75   And the cosmic hilarity of it all is we spend a full one-third of it sleeping. So if you live to be ninety, you spend thirty *years* drooling on your pillow.
76   Steven Jancey in Madison, Wisconsin, during the summer 1983. (I am, of course, making that up.)

it and sold it by now.[77] I don't have an easy solution. The best I can do is to tell you to remember how, eventually, you have moved on from virtually everyone in your life who has hurt you. It truly doesn't matter how much you loved them, how much they meant to you, or how much they were involved in your life. Eventually, over time, with clarity that comes from distance, you can move on. Think about someone you felt you couldn't live without just a few short years ago. Look at you now, all living and such. Once you realize we are made to adapt to change and handle most anything, you will wonder why you put up with so much of their shenanigans in the first place.

Take that feeling and keep it inside you. When you have trouble cutting the weight that comes with a relationship or friendship that has gone sour, remember how much better you feel when you finally do. Recall how silly you felt now that you held on for as long as you did. This is not to mean that your feelings weren't legitimate, but rather that once you overcame those feelings, you wished you had done so earlier.

Surround yourself with good people, good books, fun movies, or exercise. It's a timeworn joke about how much more in shape people get *after* a relationship ends. Yet the joke has truth to it because we often throw ourselves into something much more positive when attempting to distract ourselves. Many of those distractions are calorie free, which is a major bonus.

Don't blame yourself for making the mistakes you did, and don't project the errors of that relationship onto the next one. When you are done lifting weights, you don't take them home with you.[78] You leave them where they need to be left.[79] If that means you have to pretend certain things happened that never actually did, then so be it. What do I mean by this? Read the next quote.

---

77   And I would call it *cavoli riscaldati*, which is the Italian phrase describing the result of attempting to revive an unworkable relationship. It translates to "reheated cabbage."

78   And if you do, I think some people at Planet Fitness would like to have a talk with you.

79   Which is on the rack. Your mom doesn't work here. Clean up after yourself.

> *Life becomes easier when you learn to*
> *accept an apology you never got.*
> — Robert Brault

There's a reason why we have so many metaphors for how feelings weigh us down. Like unwanted belly fat, these emotions are literally bad for our health. In fact, bad relationships often lead to that unwanted belly fat in the first place! So by cutting off the emotional weight and letting it sink to the bottom, chances are you will look even better naked in front of mirror soon thereafter.[80] Then it's time for that quinceañera!

---

80   And Imma take your word for it.

CHAPTER 19
DEALING WITH SETBACKS

The problem with injuries is that human bodies are not like machines. Well, they aren't past the age of like eighteen, anyway. If a car breaks its, well, whatever;[81] you replace that part. After the fix, 99 percent of the time, the car works exactly the same as it did prior to that part breaking. A seamless transition allows the car to begin functioning as if nothing happened. However, if you break something in the body, once that part is healed, you have to deal with whatever step backward you have taken during the healing process.

Emotional setbacks are similar but different. Typically you haven't actually injured a part of your body, but the pain can sometimes feel much worse. However, when you are able to overcome that setback, you are often like the car in the example above: ready to roll. When someone breaks your heart, it feels like the end of the world. But when another person mends it, you jump in feetfirst and are ready to love again. Well, most of the time anyway.[82]

Professional setbacks fall into a grayer area. Depending on whether it is a minor setback, like moving the day of a meeting from a Monday to a Tuesday, a roadblock that requires a little more planning and solutions, or a defeat that leaves you scrambling for answers, there are ways to handle them all.

---

81 I love cars but don't know much about their innards. I wanna say, "Carboflux transmission"?

82 Try not to jump at people feetfirst.

Here's the thing—setbacks of all kinds suck. Even if they are minor, they can often lead you to assigning blame to things that are blameless. For example, if you are trying to get into shape and you twist your ankle, it can really curtail your desire to keep on with your "in-shape" plan. You figure that the universe is telling you to stay fat and you wouldn't have hurt yourself in the first place if you hadn't tried to mess with the cosmic balance. In fact, the majority of people who try to get into shape do not fail from their lack of desire to do so. Rather, they fail because setbacks are tremendously difficult to deal with.

Crawling your way out of a hole only to slide back some every now and then makes a person want to give up and keep sliding. Sliding is fun, even if it eventually ends in a pit of lava.[83] The thought process of "Why should I have to work so hard just to get back to where I was already, when not working hard at all is easy as pie?" can take over your brain. So, in order to keep ourselves from doing that, we have to come up with ways to make sure we can deal with setbacks. Here are a few.

INVOLVE OTHERS

Whether it is by including friends in a running group in your goals or adding more creative minds to the writing of your book or anything in between, do not go it alone. Rarely does one's plan go from A to B without detours. If others know what you are doing, they can remind you of your end goal when you slip up here and there. I often state my plans and goals publicly once I have thoroughly vetted them, have done countless hours of planning, and am just about to undertake the endeavor. I do this not because

---

83   Like quicksand, lava was something I thought I was going to have to deal with a great deal more as an adult than I have.

I seek the attention, per se,[84] but because I can therefore be held accountable. That way, on the odd chance my own motivation fails, those who wish me well will remind me of the reason I started. Or they can just simply add motivation.

They can lift you up with kind words, or a donation, or whatever it is that might be making your task a little more difficult. Like bees protecting a hive, the teamwork is what overcomes obstacles. Think I am using a metaphor without an example? Well, when giant hornets (sometimes an inch and a half long) attack Japanese honey bee hives, there is a serious problem. The honeybees' stingers can't penetrate a hornet's thick outer skin. In order to rid themselves of this dangerous menace, the bees swarm around an attacker instead, forming a spherical bee ball. Once they are in that ball, they begin vibrating their flight muscles to create heat. The mass of bees will heat the area up around the hornet to 116 degrees Fahrenheit, essentially cooking the hornet! Nature is terrifying!

From a business standpoint, this involvement of others is a crucial way to get your employees caring about the project at hand.[85] You don't need to worry about how quickly something will get implemented if the plan doesn't work, or whether people will be involved in the project at all, by thoroughly making sure those who need to be involved are invested. You can not only cut down on the setbacks that occur by having more hands involved in the creation, but you have that many more minds involved if a problem arises. It is no secret that people who are interested in the end result are more passionate about making sure something is successful.

---

84   But if I am raising awareness or money, you are darn tootin' I want attention. Self-promotion is often seen as a bad thing, but if you don't have faith in yourself, then no one will.

85   In case they have to surround a giant wasp and cook it to death.

EXPECT SETBACKS

> *Learn from the mistakes of others. You can't*
> *live long enough to make them yourself.*
> — Eleanor Roosevelt

When you realize that your straight-line planning is going to have more turns than San Francisco's Lombard Street, you will be less likely to be deterred when you hit a curve.[86] In fact, sometimes a setback will push you in a direction beneficial to your endgame. We have all dodged the bullet on a potential relationship partner who would have ended up being horrible for us. Yet we seem to forget that was a setback at the time. We lost someone we started to care for and were hurt because of that loss. But the disaster down the road would have been far worse than the heartache we initially underwent.

If you plan for the inevitable failure at some point in your grand plan, then you won't actually have a failure. Furthermore, any time lost grumbling over things not going right can be spent on plan B, which often can be a better plan in the long run. You know I have an example.

Scottish bacteriologist Alexander Fleming was known for being not particular tidy. When he came back from a vacation in 1928, he found that a green mold called *Penicillium notatum* had contaminated petri dishes in his lab which had been left out in the air. This mold was killing some of the bacteria he'd been growing in those dishes. So he isolated the mold, grew more of it, and experimented to see how many other bacteria it could kill. It turns out it was a lot of bacteria. What setback had Fleming been besot with? Just the discovery of penicillin. Years later we all learned that penicillin works by

---

86   Here is where I would like to give a shout-out to Snake Alley in Burlington, Iowa. While Lombard Street has more turns, Snake Alley has more degrees of turning (1,100 degrees to 1,000.)

preventing bacteria from forming new cell walls. With no new walls, there are no new cells and therefore no new bacterial growth. Fleming undoubtedly was ready for all sorts of odd things to happen in his petri dishes, and when something unexpected came up, even though it wasn't his initial plan, he went with a plan B. Now we live like forty years longer because of that setback.

MANAGE EXPECTATIONS

You do this by giving yourself time to process what has happened to you, not panicking, and making peace with what has happened. "Cut yourself some slack, but make sure you hold onto the rope" is a great way to imagine how you should manage expectations. Once that is done, regain control over everything. You can do this!

As a long-distance runner, I know that what I do is an exercise in injury management. The body was made to run and to run inordinately long distances. The idea that running is bad for your knees is up there with us faking the moon landing when it comes to being not only false but way more prevalent in the minds of people than it should be. The human body can do amazing things. But it is good to remember that it also has limitations. When I go into a race, I have to make sure that I know what I can realistically expect of myself. If I am trained properly, I can do X. If I am less than that, I have to manage my expectations. Many more times than not, when I toe the line, I am going to finish in a time that is slower than I wanted it to be. This is a small setback. I deal with it by making sure that I know what should happen on that day with regard to how well I can perform.

> *That was the thing about the world: it wasn't that things were harder than you thought they were going to be, it was that they were hard in ways that you didn't expect.*
> — Lev Grossman

Basically, as with all things, we simply must keep a positive attitude. Positive thoughts may not make a bone heal any more quickly or help you find the error in the code you have been working on, but negative thoughts just make you a miserable bastard to be around until you do.[87]

---

87   *Don't Be a Miserable Bastard* was almost the title of this book.

CHAPTER 20

NEVER MIND NEW YEAR'S RESOLUTIONS

It is highly unlikely you are reading this around New Year's Eve. If you are—great. If you aren't—even better, because I caught you in time to stop wasting your time on resolutions.

Actually, we shouldn't forget resolutions per se. We just shouldn't make them on January 1 because Western society has decided that will be the beginning of a new year. Rather, go ahead and make those resolutions on the first of January. Then do so again on the ninth of February. If need be, do it again on the twelfth of March. Or any day of any month throughout the year. My point is that every day should be a chance to start afresh.

> *Forget past mistakes. Forget failures. Forget everything*
> *except for what you're going to do right now and do it.*
> — Will Durant

The reason I like this quote above so much is that it addresses all we can really do at any moment in time. We can only deal with what is happening in this exact moment. We cannot lose five pounds right now.[88] We cannot have all our transgressions, faults, and foibles end immediately. We can only deal with the present. In running, especially long-distance races, there are thousands of seconds to deal with. We sometimes try to think of the race as a single entity, but each one is broken into lots of little fragments. Feel good right now? Surge! Feeling not so great at this moment? Lay off the throttle.

On New Year's Eve a few years ago, in the midst of a great deal of challenging things going on in my life, I ran a six-hour race around a one-mile loop in San Francisco's Crissy Field. I did not have the race I was hoping to but was fortunate to still post the highest total of miles run that day. That's runner parlance for "I won." However, during the race, both my mental energy and my physical energy ebbed and flowed and not from the normal wear and tear of running 41.4 miles in 6 hours. When some unexpected chafing occurred, I knew I could only deal with it at that moment. I could not think about whether it would get worse down the road.[89] All I could do was handle what was happening at that exact moment. Randomly, my mind would go blank. I would forget my woes, which were much larger than normal, and focus only on putting one foot in front of the other. Other times, my mind would race, thinking about all the things that were currently going haywire, and I would have a bad lap or two. When that would happen, I would stop worrying about the things that were mostly out of my control,[90] and I put my efforts into that which I could control.[91]

I see the New Year's resolutions that people declare as being bold and

---

88   Lest we go the Brad Pitt route in *Se7en* of "What's in the booooox?"
89   And oh, my goodness, did it, in spite of my efforts to quell the loss of skin and flesh. I still cringe a decade later at how painful that was.
90   My father's failing health was one, and a relationship coming to an abrupt end was another.
91   Somehow, less than a day after he was basically given hours to live, he rebounded. Granted, he would only live for another year, but the stubborn SOB wasn't ready to go yet.

wonderful. Unfortunately, these resolutions are often so broad and far-reaching that accomplishing them is nearly impossible. This only sets up the resolution declarer for failure. I suggest, instead, to set smaller goals and to set them daily. Each day brings its own triumphs and tribulations. Each day must be dealt with differently than the previous one. No one way of attacking life will work for every single day, just like no one way of running will work for every single race. Or no one way of writing works for every author. Or no one way of whatever will work for that subset of whatever.

If you have a bad day, realize it will be done at midnight. Then you can simply work on making that next day the one that counts. So how do you do that?

INVEST IN YOUR HEALTH

I know, I know. The guy who ran fifty-two marathons in a year is telling you to put your health as a priority. Shocking, right? But I can tell you from firsthand experience how valuable it is. I played collegiate rugby and was a much bigger person then as a twenty-year-old than I am twenty-plus years later. After college ended, that weight, all 235 pounds of it, did not stay in the realm of fitness. I was hardly morbidly obese, but I was hefty. As such, much in my life suffered because I was not concerned about my waistline as much as I am now. But when I talk about your health, it is about so much more than just eating properly.

We are sleeping less and less as a society. That lack of sleep causes major problems not only in our interpersonal lives but in our productivity as employees or business owners. While we all think about sleeping more, we should really be thinking about sleeping better. Don't lie in bed with your phone looking at things that absolutely do not need your attention. Also, if you use the phone as an alarm, put it far away so you aren't tempted to look at it in the middle of the night. Like in another room. That way you won't hit the snooze (which also does nothing to help you at all and is a horrible invention).

Drink some freaking water, people. Also, unless you literally live in a place like Flint, Michigan,[92] drink your tap water. Bottled water is less regulated than tap water; it is wasteful plastic, and the companies that make it are sucking up water resources from the places that actually need it. Regardless of where you get it, however, drink it! Your body is begging you to drink more water. Water curbs hunger. Water revitalizes you. Water is calorie free! What more can you want?[93]

Stop smoking. Stop drinking alcohol. They are both poisons. I know you wine drinkers like to talk about antioxidants and whatnot and this one little paragraph is not going to convince you otherwise,[94] but if you want to live a better life, stop abusing your body. It is the only one you have. Treat it as such.

Surround yourself with good people. Your mental and emotional health are just as important as your physical health. Our bodies are so intertwined with our feelings and our thoughts that neglecting any one of them makes it harder to live a good life. You want a resolution that really matters? Then start with the decision not to hamstring yourself in every aspect of your life by not taking care of you first.

REALIGN YOUR LONG-TERM GOALS

For thirty years I had done everything in my life to try to gain one goal: to be an officer in the CIA. I didn't smoke, drink, do drugs, or do anything else that would keep me from getting this goal. I first got a bachelor's degree and then a law degree in my pursuit of hopefully becoming a spy. I then began the interview process with not only the CIA but the Secret Service, DEA, and FBI as well. To make a long story short, I never fully realized this

---

92   And unfortunately, places "like Flint, Michigan" are growing.
93   OK, maybe a Lamborghini Countach like the one on the poster in your wall in the late '80s. No? Just me? Liars.
94   I bet a whole book won't convince many of you.

dream with any of these agencies despite going deep into the process of making that happen.

As such, I concluded that even though all I had ever known was this one goal, it wasn't going to come to fruition. I needed to adjust my desires and find something new that I could become passionate about. This didn't happen immediately. But that's how I started a career in the running industry.

It began when I convinced a company in Utah that they were lacking a certain position and that I alone could fill that position. Subsequently, I went from being inches away from working for Uncle Sam to picking up my entire life and moving to Salt Lake City designing superlong racecourses. Soon thereafter I branched out on my own. Now, I was a full-fledged speaker, talking to people at races across the country about my running feats. I became an author, sharing tales of my adventures with even more people. After about a decade in that arena, I saw some changes coming and realized that I needed to once again stay ahead of the curve by changing what I did on a daily basis.

So I made a switch away from doing speaking engagements at running expos in the athletic world and went more toward corporate gigs in that realm. I tailored my life's experiences to speak to land title associations, economic summits, real estate conventions, small schools, big universities, and everything else you can possibly imagine. Each one of these changes was not something I necessarily wanted to do. But by seeing the changes that were coming (and always having one small back burner lit in order to cook up a new career just in case I need to switch career paths), I was ready for the changes that came. The folder of potentials I had in my head of what I might have to do when that situation arose kept me from floundering when it did.

Now you needn't change your entire career or move across the country (and then do it three more times) in order to realign your goals. But you change as you age. Your desires change. You add family members. You make new friends. You lose desires in one area and gain them in another. You are a constantly evolving mass of thoughts and emotions and firing synapses.

Why should you still have the same hopes and dreams at thirty (or forty or fifty or sixty) that you did as a teenager? Everything changes, and you should evolve with it.

GAIN EMPATHY

One thing that limits us as human beings more than virtually anything else is the ability to accurately understand the feelings and needs of others. We only live in our own heads, and even that is sometimes scary. Figuring out our own desires is hard enough, but appreciating what other people are going through is the most difficult task in the world. Why? Because every single one of the seven billion people on this planet is the key player in their own drama. You are, at best, a supporting actor. You can't possibly know how to deal with everyone or know what their dreams and thoughts are at all times. So, instead, start by realizing that you can't understand it. Ask questions. Do your best to make no assumptions. Sure, generalizations exist for a reason—they are often true. But if you can also take into account that specificities also matter and tell those with whom you are dealing that their own perspective does have an impact on how you think and feel, you are already three steps ahead of most people.

It is difficult sometimes to do, but remembering the "golden rule" that we should treat others as we wish to treated is the best way to start every interaction every day of your life. You just have to remember that not everyone else follows this practice. But you can't control them. You can only master what you do yourself. It might seem like a lot of effort to not only have feelings but also share them with people so they know what you are thinking. Imagine, on the other hand, how much time and energy you will save in the long term when you aren't having to redo so many interactions in life because of misunderstandings. Suddenly the time adds up, and without wasting any of it on apologies for missteps that never needed to happen, you are suddenly finding yourself with an abundance of extra daylight in your life.

You might not get credit for it. It might be difficult. But it is the right thing to do, and you will feel better for it.

ADD ADVENTURE

Not everyone can jet off to Reykjavik.[95] But adventure can be found completely free all around us. I've been a frugal person most of my life. Most of that started with simply having absolutely nothing to spend when growing up. Whether that is what has kept me as such into adulthood or not, I remain that way to this day. Doing so, however, has afforded me the opportunity to have additional money on hand to go on adventures.

I once talked to a friend who was curious how I could spend the money that I do going places. I pointed out to them that their twice-a-day before-and-after-work Starbucks habit was costing something along the lines of $1,500 a year. This didn't even mention that they also had to burn off an additional twelve pounds of calories a year that I did not by not doing the exact same thing. By avowing just one little thing, I was basically putting enough money in my pocket to pay for at least a couple of trips to faraway places.

That said, as I mentioned, you don't even have to save money to enjoy life. You can explore thrift stores and yard sales. You can check out cheap or free entertainment in your town from local theaters or musicians. You can go to museums or libraries or so many other things that cost a fraction of what many people spend by eating their lunches and dinners at restaurants all the time. I'm not saying that you should give up every single creature comfort. I get that sometimes that five-dollar mixed Frappuccino is the only thing that's going to get you through that meeting at work. I'm simply saying that it adds up over time.

---

95   But, seriously, you really should.

> *Dynamite is loyal to the one who lights the fuse.*
> — Dean F. Wilson

Regardless, adventure will knock your cobwebs off, invigorate your soul, and should be a solid part of your life moving forward. You needn't plan every weekend around some brand-spanking-new excursion. In fact, staying home can be an adventure if you decide to try a new hobby like finally giving painting a whirl or putting those poems you have in your head down on paper. The crux of the issue is that you must cultivate your soul with fresh ideas and actions lest you stagnate, wither, and blow away.

CHAPTER 21
ENJOY THE VIEW

> *The moment of victory is much too short*
> *to live for that and nothing else.*
> — Martina Navratilova[96]

When we have goals, especially big ones, it is hard not to envision the moment when they are completed and what will happen when we finally achieve our dreams. We expect that we will have feelings of elation, that trumpets will blare, and that the world will stop for us, even if just for an hour or so. The reality is, for the most part, few of those things ever occur.[97]

Traveling home from my solo running of the 202-mile American Odyssey Relay, I had an overwhelming sense of melancholy. I have often experienced similar dips in emotion postmarathon, so this was nothing new. But it was a little deeper this time and held on a little bit longer. Even though I had accomplished one of the hardest things I have ever done in my life, no giant fireworks went off, no wonderful feelings flowed through my veins for hours on end, and the finality of the moment was brought up immediately

---

96   I'd like to add that Martina once retweeted me. Can we put that in my obituary?
97   I always carry a trumpet just in case. That way I can get at least one.

with questions like "So what's next?"[98]

I was reading a book on the plane home the next day called *Harriers.* A nonfiction account about a high school cross-country team in Salem, Ohio, this book was a gripping tale of a team that had done nothing for an extremely long time before coming out of nowhere to win the state title. There was a passage in it about an individual state champion in some sport speaking about how fleeting his moment of success was and how quickly people would either stop caring about his title or just simply forget. The point was that with a team effort, people will still forget, but at least you and your team can savor the memory together.

This book, coupled with my own feelings of blahness postrace, really drove home the quote I started this chapter with from tennis great Martina Navratilova. I know my own feelings were partially stemming from achieving something I had been planning for two years and the subsequent weight lifted upon successively doing so. But more than that, the emotions I was experiencing were a reminder that we have to enjoy the journey, not just the destination. Doing so is sometimes laboriously difficult in our goal-oriented world.

There is nothing wrong with having high standards and acquiring a single-minded purpose when in the midst of trying to achieve them. At the same time, we also have to embrace the ability to back off once in a while, stop the rush forward, and check out what we have accomplished along the way. Will that stop the postmarathon blues, so to speak? Probably not. Sometimes we have to focus on an endpoint in a task in order to get through it. But many times, with no end in sight, you have to be in the now. For 50 hours and 15 minutes of my 202-mile run mentioned above, I could not picture the finish line. Not because I couldn't think of it but because I knew I *shouldn't* think of it. It was an unfathomable amount of distance away. I

---

98   I mean, like *immediately* immediately. Even quicker than the fifty-two marathon phone call I mentioned earlier. Standing at the finish line, being interviewed, and caught on camera for the documentary *No Handoffs*, I literally had to say, "I'm gonna sit down."

was going to be running for two straight days plus more.[99] Only in that last few seconds could I finally allow myself to imagine being done. I tried my best to enjoy the sights along the way during the run, but mostly I had to have tunnel vision as I inched forward. This allowed me to not worry about the finish and, every once in a while, turn to my crew and say, "Damn, that view is gorgeous."

As cliché as it sounds, enjoying the view makes everything better. For example, if you see exercise as just a means to an end, you are never really going to be fit enough, or fast enough, or strong enough. But if you understand that small steps increase your overall health, allow you to learn new things about your body, and give you the opportunity to push yourself further than ever before, that hour a day you spend sweating becomes a part of your life you look forward to, rather than slogging through. Similarly, if you want to learn a new language but are only focused on becoming proficient enough to make it through the vacation you have saved for years for, then you will miss all the subtle intricacies that make each language so unique. Languages are more than just conveyances of ideas but are shared stories created over hundreds of years. Delving into the meanings behind words and the reasons why they are said in what manner makes the language come to life. Suddenly verb tense and the appropriate article for whichever gendered noun aren't nearly as cumbersome!

Allow me another personal story to help drive home this point. A few years back, I put together a plan to run the length of the Panama Canal. A bit over fifty miles long, the distance of the Panama Canal itself is something I can do with relative ease if trained properly. There is an elevation change that would add some difficulty to it, and without a doubt, the heat and humidity would make it a challenge for me. But to traverse the canal was something I had wished to do for quite some time. The impetus to do so began as a joke when a friend of mine had just finished running from California to New

---

99   The original plan was closer to sixty-five hours. Everything just went so unbelievably well that it ended up being much shorter.

York in a few months' time. I said I could run from the Pacific to the Atlantic in like a third of a day and be home by dinner, so what was the big deal? Sure enough, the Panama Canal route would let me do so.

The idea finally came to fruition when another friend of mine was planning on running a trail race in Nicaragua. I decided to join them, run this trail race, and then drive through Costa Rica to Panama, taking a few days to get there and recover from the trail race. Upon completing the run in Panama, we would drive back through Costa Rica, spend a few days exploring the coast, and then get back to Nicaragua and fly home. To cut to the chase, we never left Nicaragua.

The race took place on an island comprised of two volcanos[100] in Lake Nicaragua and left us beyond decimated from the heat and humidity. As we ate dinner in one of the few places to grab food on this island, we were speaking to a local from Costa Rica who had also run the race. Different nationalities meant nothing to tired runners swapping stories, and we were thoroughly enjoying each other's company. My plan to run across Panama came up, and the Costa Rican inquired how we planned to get there from here. I mentioned we would simply take the rental car we had with us. At this point, a concerned look came over his face, and he informed us we could not take the rental car across the border into Costa Rica. As we sat mouths agape in stunned silence, he explained the only way we could do so with a car that was rented, given laws for border crossings. In order to actually cross the border, we would have to leave the car we had at the border of Costa Rica, grab all our stuff, and walk across the border. Then we would need to procure another rental car in Costa Rica, and drive it to the Panama border. Once there, we would return the car, gather our things again, and cross into Panama on foot again. Then we could grab a car in Panama. To come back to Nicaragua, we would have to repeat this process in reverse.[101] (Cue sad trombone music followed by dumbfounded stares, followed by swearing at

---

100   One of which is active. Seriously, this race is a tale unto itself.
101   This was *not* what Hertz had told us when we inquired.

the rental car company, which had previously told us this would not be a problem.)

Suffice it to say this was the last thing I wanted to do for something that was just more or less a frivolous athletic endeavor. There were too many things that could go wrong for someone who didn't speak Spanish, and it was already a tight timetable for us to do what we wanted and not get stuck in Central America. Instead, crestfallen, we changed our flights to fly back home the next day. No Costa Rica, no exploring, no Panama Canal route, and a bevy of lost hotel fees.

> *Success is walking from failure to failure*
> *with no loss of enthusiasm.*
> — Winston Churchill

I look back at that experience as the perfect example of how I not only didn't even get to start the thing that had been my goal, but I also obviously didn't finish it. Instead, I try to relive the memories of the things that went right on the journey. I was able to go to a country I had never previously visited, run in an unbelievably beautiful yet hostile environment, and bring over fifty pairs of running shoes of my own to give to the extremely destitute citizens of the Ometepe Island. This doesn't even get into the adventure that we went on when we took a wrong turn leaving Managua, Nicaragua, trying to get down to Ometepe in the first place.[102] In other words, while many years later I still have not completed that run across Panama, that trip remains a perfect example of how allowing myself to enjoy the view kept what could have been a disaster into a lifelong good story.

That has hardly been the only trip I have taken that has instilled in me

---

102 Trust me when I say it involves driving on a road that 100 percent wasn't meant to be driven on for an insanely lengthy period of time and dealing with temperamental burros.

a desire to not only enjoy the view but to always have as many backup plans as possible. I enjoy spontaneity, but I still now try to get at least different confirmations on something that might throw my plans out the window.

But if they do, I try my best to look out the window at the view.

CHAPTER 22
IGNORE THE IMPOSSIBLE

> *Tell the audience what you're going to say, say it;*
> *then tell them what you've said.*
> — Dale Carnegie

When I first heard this quote, mostly often used for public speaking, I thought it was insulting to the listeners. My original thoughts were that it insinuated the audience was so full of dullards that they needed to be told the same thing three times in order to comprehend it. I wondered how anyone who was paid any amount of money to bring a message to people could get away with this without sounding both repetitive and condescending.

Over time I came to realize that I feel Carnegie meant something completely different. Instead of repetitiveness, the first part of this maxim actually meant to simply frame the overarching theme of what was to follow. The second part was not simple repetition, but rather now that you have laid the groundwork, fill in the blanks. Finally, instead of a simple recap of what you said, you hit key points again to drive home their meaning, hopefully adding a striking final thought as well. For example, if describing the movie *Jaws*, you wouldn't say "This movie is about a fearless killer machine. Check out how he killed. Remember how he's been killing since the start?" Instead, you would lay the groundwork for the uncontrollability of nature and how man often makes bad decisions based on finance and pride issues (the mayor and local businessman refusing to close the beach thing) while reminding the audience that man is part of nature too![103] Ta-da!

Then again, I could be wrong with my interpretation of what Carnegie meant, but if I am, well, I am fairly certain my way is better anyway. Let's hear it for hubris!

Having said all of that, the impetus for this book has always been about trying to fill a need. A great deal of my writing in my life has been rather reactionary. One of the first ever entries I wrote on my website was a description on how to run a certain one-hundred-mile race. I found the literature out there on how to tackle this ultramarathon to be rather lacking, and I felt one shouldn't have to sift through race reports to glean a tidbit of info here and there. I had battled through the race with very little to go on in terms of preparation. To give firsthand info to others who couldn't train on the course or didn't personally know someone who had done so, I wrote a lengthy entry on what the course was like and my recommendations on how any runner could take on the race. I think it was rather nice of me, to be quite honest.

One of the reasons I wrote a book about must-run races all over North America was that I was tired of seeing the same list of about ten races people always felt were can't-miss. You only have to hear about the most famous races in the world a few times before you realize they sort of have a lock on the media coverage. To me, these lists were doing a disservice to runners out there who want to experience originality but don't have the funds or time to research all the different venues. If I could provide some insight into races that they may never have heard of, then I was helping my fellow runners enjoy the world more. Again, damn, I am a nice guy.

Similarly, upon reading so many advice columns and inspirational tomes that I felt were sorely lacking, I wanted to do what I could to say what they weren't saying. *Ignore the Impossible* was never just a motto. It was a way

---

103   If you ever need to know how forgiving humans are, remember that mayor in *Jaws* was still the mayor in *Jaws 2*.

of life that I have been living for quite some time. Not too long ago, I was presented with a memory on social media from someone showing what I had written to them in my first book. Sure enough, I told them they should do one thing: *Ignore the Impossible.*

I promise you I am not a Pollyanna starry-eyed optimist. I am often frustrated with the way my life has taken turns that make it more difficult. I never ask "Why me?" because, really, "Why not me?" But I do wonder when some things will finally break my way. However, when those feelings of being overwhelmed start to take over, or I question whether the time needed to accomplish my tasks or desires is worth it, I remember how far I have come.

> *Never give up on a dream just because of the time it will take to accomplish it; time will pass anyway.*
> — Earl Nightingale

The passage of time only exists because we humans need to know when to eat dinner or when *Matlock* is on.[104] It is an odd construct but one we have created to understand how to get through our days. Any way you see it, though, each person has the exact same amount of time each day to do with what they want. Twenty-four hours pass between the start of one day and the start of the next. What you are going to do with those twenty-four hours remains the only question.

I was a history major in college. As a student of times that have passed, I often marveled at how relatively short time periods shaped the course of human history. The United States was brought into World War II with just days left in 1941. Three years later the war was over. The people involved had no idea what they would have to suffer through for the next one thousand days. Here in the future, that period doesn't, at first blush, seem like the

---

104   It is always 4:30 p.m.

longest amount of time to suffer through. But the problem with living in the present and looking back at the past is how much that prism distorts the experiences of those who lived through it. If you hit your thumb with a hammer, the next few minutes are going to be the worst of your life, yet in the future, you probably won't even give it a second thought.

That's why one should never allow difficult times to stop them from pursing what it is that they desire. The task may seem like it will take a long time, but as is often said, a year from now, you will wish you began today. What you must reconcile in your head is the fact that what you want may possibly never occur. But unless you take the steps now to put your plans into motion, you can all but guarantee you will never get what you are hoping to get your grabby hands on.

> *Trust because you are willing to accept the*
> *risk, not because it's safe or certain.*
> — Anonymous

Everything in life is a risk. Every step could break an ankle, but every step could have you discovering a precious artifact. Every breath could be your last, but every breath could also be the one where your life is fulfilled. If you do nothing, you are guaranteed to die anyway. If you do as much as you can, you will still die eventually, but along the way, you will have lived. You will have experienced. You will have learned and loved. You will have given and taken. You will have hopefully left a better world for those who follow you and maybe even a small legacy to a few people.

We have so little control over so much that happens to us on a daily basis. But we can absolutely control how we react to it. No one is going to react to any situation the same way as another person. We are complex, interesting creatures who have our own unique spin on every single second that happens to us. Based on our DNA, our upbringing, or whether we were hungry right then or not, we can expect to be presented with a variety of emotions and reactions to that which happens around us. While we are not complete masters of every involuntary action, we can learn to guide our ships through even the choppiest of waters. Like a wizened sea captain piloting his vessel deftly between jagged rocks hidden by a tossed sea, the only way you can keep your own ship afloat is unfortunately, by taking a few blows to the hull along the way.

The tired phrase "No one said it would be easy; they just said it would be worth it" irks me. No one said it would be worth it either. In fact, in reality, for many people, a great deal of the time, life seems not only hard, but the worth is hard to see. The world is full of terrible things: strife, war, famine, pestilence, ignorance, hunger, pain, sickness, and death.

But it is also full of so many wonderful things: laughter, love, pizza, the smell of rain on hot pavement, and the twinkling in the eye of someone we care about. Most importantly, with regard to moving your own goals forward, what matters most is that that your life has *you* in it. It is not selfish to realize that your world has one absolute: you. What are you going to do with that knowledge?

If anything, I hope this book will have taught you one thing: regardless of what has been put in front of you, what has helped you, what has hindered you, what you want, what you need, what is fighting you, or what is helping you, it is absolutely amazing what you can achieve if you do one simple thing.

Ignore the impossible.

ACKNOWLEDGMENTS

There are so many people I would like to thank who have made this book a reality. My family is at the top of that list, as they undoubtedly have made it clear to me what it means to throw caution to the wind and never allow obstacles to get in your way. Without them I wouldn't be the man I am today.

The following had a huge hand in making this book come to fruition, and I would be remiss to not take the time to thank all of them: John R. Hanson, John Roman, Pete Eisenmann, Bob Merrill, Christine Lauer, Emmanuel Moustakakis, Jessica Terrien, Danny Fleener, Jenny Rutherford, Ross Kinney, Lonnie Somers, Miguel Cuadrado, Kris Graci, Mentha Benek, Felix DuBosse, Damaris Rosich-Schwartz, Jason Zacher, Manfred Schmidt, Kevin Newton, Drew Hamilton Butler, Jeff Bockhorn, Shari L. Davis, Chris Johnson, Brandon Cumby, Jen Reed, Erin Thompson, William B. Latter, Heather Alvarado Rine, Anurup Joseph, John Mehall, Bob Jennings, John Titus, Jessica Thurber, Mark Lindsley, Lane Blake, Elizabeth Granoff, Stefan Wagner, Vincent Reedy, Dave McGillivray, Heidi Maldonado, Grant Crampton, Gwen Jacobson, Todd Sailer, Tristan Pretty, John P. ßarti, Richard Gibson, Troy Vaupel, Richelle Richardson, Daun Lyon, Jaci VanScooter, Tony Huffman, and Lindsay Jameson.

Finally, to those who have read and enjoyed my previous books, articles, blogs, and random musings, thank you very much for coming back for more.

I always try to do better.